CILLA
BLACK
Step Inside

CILLA BLACK

Step Inside

RETRO CLASSICS
is a collection of facsimile reproductions
of popular bestsellers from the 1980s and 1990s

Step Inside first published in 1985 by J.M. Dent & Sons Ltd

Re-issued in 2015 as a Retro Classic
by G2 Entertainment
in association with Lennard Publishing
Windmill Cottage
Mackerye End
Harpenden
Hertfordshire
AL5 5DR

ISBN 978-1-78281-995-0

Editor Michael Leitch
Cover design by David Pocknell's Company Ltd

The publishers would like to thanks the following
for their help in providing illustrations:

Illustrators
John Ireland - Lady on the Rocks, Doris's Girl, Family and Friends
Roy Knipe - When Ignorance Was Bliss, The Cutting-Room Floor
Paul Leith - Are You Anybody?, Australia
Justin Swarbrick - Time Off in Austria
Joe Wright - Mersey Roots, The Joy of Flying, A Place of our Own

Picture Acknowledgements
BBC Photographs, Sarah Evans, Hatton Photo Features, Liverpool Daily Post & Echo,
London Weekend Television, David Magnus, The Photo Source, Rex Features, Peter
Shirley/Daily Express, Syndication International

Printed and bound by Ingrams Lightning Source

This book is a facsimile reproduction of the first edition of
Step Inside which was a bestseller in 1985.
No attempt has been made to alter any of the wording
with the benefit of hindsight, or to update the book in any way.

CONTENTS

MERSEY ROOTS

*'Liverpool people say such funny things,
I can't gerrem out of me 'ead.'*

It's true. People ask me to explain it, and I can't, at least not so it makes one single, harmonious glob of sense. What I do know is, whenever I go back there or meet Liverpool people, they have me in fits.

Their humour is certainly down to earth. Nothing makes the lower deck of a Liverpool bus laugh more than the sight of someone else running to catch the bus and missing it. The closer they get, the funnier it is. Best of all, the feller comes flying down the street, reaches out and gets one hand on the pole, but the bus is

pulling away from him and he can't get in his jump and land on the platform. His legs are spinning round like catherine wheels, but the bus is winning, then one foot trips over the other and suddenly his legs are trailing out behind him in the road. Even the conductor is laughing by now, but when the feller's hand begins to slip down the pole, the whole bus is in hysterics.

It's a hard school, but that's the way we are. Terrible stories come off the building sites. Bobby's brother Bertie had a friend called Barney Williams. In those days the lime used for making mortar was kept in troughs. As the lime settled, water came to the surface and this had to be siphoned off with a tube. One day, three or four fellers had a go at sucking the water up through the tube but nothing came out. They decided to ask Barney.

'Ey, Barney. Can you do this?'

Barney gave the tube an almighty suck. Whoop! Up jumped a piece of lime and went straight down Barney's throat and into his stomach. In no time he was rolling around on the floor. It could have killed him. Someone sent for an ambulance, and he was rushed off to hospital and given a stomach pump. But before the ambulance came, all his mates did was stand there roaring with laughter.

There's a famous local radio programme called the *Billy Butler Show,* and he has a hilarious quiz spot where the audience phones in and has to answer silly questions. If they're stuck, they shout: 'Gissa clue, Billy,' and Billy tries to help out – but not always.

One of his questions was: 'What was Hitler's first name?' Well, it had this poor woman floored from the start. 'Gissa clue, Billy!' she pleaded.

'Now, come on,' he said, 'I can't give you a clue for that. Everyone knows the answer. I tell you what, I'll play some music while you go and ask a neighbour.'

So he played a bit of music, and came back to the woman on the phone.

'Have you thought about it?' he asked her.

'Yes,' she said. 'It's alright. I know it now.'

'Fine,' said Billy. 'What was Hitler's first name?'

She said: 'Heil!'

Another time, he played a record by Tight Fit called *The Lion Sleeps Tonight.* After he'd played it, he gave the title again and asked:

'Now, who made that record a Number One?'

'Oh, gissa clue, Billy! Gissa clue!'

'Well,' he said, 'think of your husband's underpants.'

'I've got it, Billy!' she shouted. 'It's the Dooleys.'

Then Billy went back to the first-name game. 'What was the first name

8

of Christ?' he wanted to know.

'Now don't tell me,' said the feller. 'I know him. Just give us a second.'

A few seconds went by, and all anyone could hear from the feller was confused muttering.

'Are you still working on it?' Billy asked him.

'Yes,' said the feller. 'Don't tell me. He's the Son of God.' Then the feller started muttering again. 'Jesus Christ,' he said to himself, 'what's his name?'

****

Liverpool people also have a funny way of taking things very literally – especially if they are unsure of themselves. Hospitals can be confusing places and a lot of funny things happen there. In fact, I almost wonder if the doctors don't make hospitals mysterious on purpose, so people will do what they are told and shurrup.

Me Dad went into hospital. He was very nervous, and just sat on his bed until the nurse came round. She reached in her basket and tossed him a couple of white objects.

'Slip this over your head,' she said and vanished out the door.

Unfortunately, there had been a mix-up in the laundry, and when she came back she found Dad had put them on – but they weren't robes for wearing in bed, they were pillow-cases. He had one pulled down over his head and we think the other one was round his feet. Poor Dad. If only he'd watched his *Dr Kildare* more carefully.

My mother was watching a programme on television about geriatrics and how they were looked after. It was a sad programme, all these old people shuffling about in a home, or just staring out the window. My mother said to me:

'Oh, I hope I don't end up like that.' Then she looked at me. 'Promise you won't ever put me in a home.' She raised her head. 'I'd rather have Anastasia.'

They are the same in Bobby's family. His brother Kenny went to see the doctor about his varicose veins. The doctor said:

'Take your trousers off and get on the table.'

Kenny pulled off his trousers, climbed on the table and stood on it! The doctor looked surprised, but Kenny said it all made sense to him at the time:

'You get varicose veins from too much standing, right? Well, that's how I showed him me legs. Stood up.'

Liverpool was much more of an island-by-the-Mersey than it is now. People are still very independent in their minds, but the borders have grown

9

STEP INSIDE

a bit blurred with the extra housing and the overflow developments like they built at Kirkby. Since The Beatles, everyone and his dog wants to say they're from Liverpool, but a lot of them aren't. The real Liverpool is the area inside the city limits. It's not Bootle, which is a small town – with its own Town Hall – surrounded by the City of Liverpool. Bootle people, to be fair to them, always say they are from Bootle; they aren't interested in being part of Liverpool.

The people on the other side of the water are definitely not Liverpool. They are foreigners. Anyone from New Brighton, Wallasey, Moreton and the other towns across the Mersey belongs to a race apart.

Imagine what it was like in those days to leave Liverpool and travel to somewhere like . . . London! The first time I was in a Royal Command performance, me Dad and our family (the Whites) went down to London by train with Bobby's brothers and their wives (the Willises). On the journey the men all went along to the bar, leaving the women in the compartment. A waiter came along with a trolley and asked if they would like coffee.

'Yes, please,' they all said.

'Are you all white?' he asked.

'Oh no,' said a Liverpool voice. 'Three of us are Willis.'

They had a wonderful outing. They were booked into the Mayfair Hotel, then Bobby took his brothers to Moss Brothers to hire their evening suits. Well, the brothers were new men once they had the suits on. One of them said he felt like James Bond, and they kept wearing them for twelve hours – from four o'clock in the afternoon, when they first went to the shop, through till the show started at seven, and afterwards till they got to bed at about four in the morning.

They didn't see me, of course. I only had one song, *You're My World*. Our families were much too busy staring into the Royal Box to pay me any attention. They had seats in the Circle and were on the same level as the Royal Family. They were enchanted. Whenever the Queen applauded, they did. They never took their eyes off her. After the show I asked them how they thought my act had gone.

They said: 'Which one were you?'

Unfortunately, we never heard about this until much later, but Bobby's brother lost his job because of that weekend. His boss had forbidden him to go and he had taken no notice.

'I'm going down to the Royal Command,' he said firmly, 'to see me sister-in-law.'

The boss said: 'You can't go.'

'I'm going.'

'If you go, you'll lose your job.'

10

These pictures were taken while I was filming for my TV series on Liverpool's practice ground in 1971. As you can see in the photo with Bill Shankly, I wore the No 9 shirt – which actually belonged to Ian St John – and later in the day I put a penalty past Ray Clemence. The other players training with me and Jimmy Tarbuck are, from the left, John Toshack, Larry Lloyd, Ian Callaghan, Brian Hall, Peter Thompson and Steve Heighway.

'Well, I'm going.'

So he went – and he did lose his job. If only we had known about it earlier, we might have been able to help. But we didn't. Poor Bertie. It cost him his job to sit and look at the Queen.

Another time in London, while I was at the Palladium, Bobby and I took me Mum, Dad and Auntie Nellie to what was then the in-club to go to – Danny La Rue's in Hanover Square. When we got there, we had a very nice table and Danny, when he came on, introduced me to the rest of the guests. That was a bit special for my parents, and I could see they were proud that I had been recognized in a posh place like this night club.

Then, just towards the end of Danny's act, me Dad leaned over very slowly and quietly to Bobby and muttered out of the corner of his mouth, indicating the stage: 'Don't tell the girls. But that girl's a feller.'

Bobby looked at me Dad, and he was perfectly serious. So Bobby thought he'd better not say: 'Well, yes, we all know that.' He decided to seem surprised instead, so he raised his eyebrows and said: 'Is he?'

Me Dad nodded. 'I've been away to sea,' he said, 'and I know these things.'

✱✱✱✱

Liverpool men all take their football very seriously, and the boys are even worse. Barney Williams, who sucked the lime through the tube, was a demon footballer – especially when his dad was watching him.

He was playing in the street with some of his mates. They played between the lamp posts with a tennis ball. If it was a corner-kick, they used to throw the ball in from the side so it would be high enough for them to head into goal. One day they were waiting for a corner to be taken when Barney's dad came out of the pub.

'Ere, lads,' he said. 'Give that to me. I'll take the corner.'

He bent down to pick up the ball, but instead, for a joke, he picked up half a brick. Now, everyone saw him pick up the brick, but they thought they'd let Barney's dad have his bit of fun, so nobody said anything.

'Ere you go,' he called, and lobbed the brick across.

All the boys stood back of course – except for Barney. He couldn't get it out of his brains that *his Dad* was taking a *corner-kick*. So he went for it. Thud! It nearly took his head off. Another example of a Liverpudlian being literal-minded. Of course, some would say he was a bit of a Richard Cranium.

That is a real Liverpool original. I first heard it from a girl while we were up there filming for *Surprise Surprise*.

'Oh,' she said, after telling me about something embarrassing that had just happened to her, 'I felt a real Richard Cranium.'

'Richard Cranium?' I said.

'Yerr,' she said. 'Don't yer know it? Dickhead.'

Afterwards, Bobby said he wanted to use it on the paging system at London Weekend Television. It hasn't happened yet, but our friends in the know can't wait to hear the announcement:

'Will Mr Richard Cranium please report to Reception.'

Sometimes Liverpool is more like *Boys From The Blackstuff*. Life is hard there for a lot of people, and they just reckon it would be a lot worse if they didn't laugh. The time Bobby's brother Bertie gave up driving a taxi is a good example.

He was sitting on the rank on a slow day. Business was very poor and it was taking an age for the drivers to move up to the head of the rank. Eventually, after maybe two hours, he got there and then his customer arrived. He was an old man and he shuffled up to the rank in one of those walking frames.

Bertie got out to give him a hand, and a heavy smell of booze hit him.

''Ere you are, Pop,' said Bertie. He took the walking frame off him and helped him into the cab. As he climbed in, the old man vomited over Bertie's jacket.

'Ugh!' went Bertie. 'Look at that. You dirty old . . . Get in there.'

Bertie went round the front, took off his jacket and rolled it up carefully. He got into the driving seat and turned his head.

'Where yer going?' he asked.

The old man said: 'Round the corner.'

'Great,' thought Bertie. 'That's all I need – a two-hour wait and then this cripple comes along, pukes all over me jacket and wants a 2s.6d. fare.' He thought seriously of flinging him out and waiting for a better fare. Then he thought: 'No. He's a cripple. Poor old devil.'

Bertie by now had mixed feelings about his disabled customer. Eventually he took him round the corner to his destination, stopped the cab, got out, opened the rear door, helped the old man out, stood him on the pavement and helped him back inside his walking frame.

'That'll be two and six,' said Bertie.

'Get stuffed,' said the old man, and pushed off.

It was Bertie's last ride – or nearly. He drove round the next corner and joined the back of the taxi queue, then fumed until it was time to go home. Later he announced that he was giving up driving taxis.

'I'm not doing that again,' he said. 'I'm not working for the public any more. Not after that. The public? I can't stand them!'

13

WHEN
IGNORANCE
WAS BLISS

'There was a time I didn't know where I was going next until I read it in the New Musical Express.'

In the old days everything was much less organized. Agents never saw themselves as any thing more than bookers. They'd hand you a list of dates for the week, and after that you were on your own. You found your own way from A to B and booked your own hotel. It didn't occur to the agents to do more because in their eyes pop singers didn't count for much. Apart from Helen Shapiro, Tommy Steele, Cliff Richard and maybe a couple of others, the life of a pop singer was very short. You could reel off dozens of names of people who had two hits and then vanished.

14

Brian Epstein was the first to organize a complete management package. He saw the investment possibilities, and the people who signed for him got a lot of extra services – press agent, travel agent, secretarial help with letters, and a general feeling that here was someone who would look after you.

Before Brian came along, we wallowed in our ignorance, and only learnt things by experience. On my first theatre date we arrived at the Odeon in Southport and the stage manager asked Bobby for his lighting plot, which is the plan of all the lights needed for my act.

'Where's yer plot?' he said.

'Yes,' said Bobby, who didn't know what he was talking about but wanted to be helpful. 'Yes, it is hot, isn't it?'

'No,' said the stage manager. 'Yer plot. I need yer plot.'

'Me what?' asked Bobby.

And so on for several years while I made the transition from being someone who sang at parties and in clubs to being a solo singer in theatres. For those early dates my backing band was anyone else on the bill. At Coventry the Fourmost helped me out. They'd been on already, so they had the great idea of blacking up to try and disguise themselves. We put the lights really low, but it didn't fool the fans who gave them a barracking, but all in fun. Life seemed much more innocent in 1963.

Another thing I should have had, but didn't, was my own sheet music so that different bands could accompany me. Even Brian Epstein didn't realize this, because he was only used to handling groups. I actually went down to London to do *Saturday Club* on radio with Brian Matthew. The resident band was Bob Miller and the Millermen.

Bob Miller asked: 'What are you going to do for the show?'

I said: 'I want to do *Love of the Loved* which Paul McCartney has written for me.'

'Fine,' he said. 'Where are your parts?'

'Parts?' I said. I couldn't think what he meant.

'Yes,' he said. 'Parts. Your music.'

'Are you crazy?' I said. 'You don't know this song? It's being played on the radio every five minutes!'

I couldn't understand his problem. When I performed with rock and roll bands, they'd pick up a new tune in about five minutes and then we'd do it. Suddenly I'm in a BBC studio and they want it all written out.

So then Bobby had a go. 'Look,' he said, 'I've got a copy of the record here. And I've got this.' He produced a portable record player, opened the lid and played *Love of the Loved*. 'There you are!' he said.

Bob Miller was very kind, and very patient – if he hadn't been, I might have gone straight back to Liverpool. 'Yes,' he said. 'I know. Playing the record to me is one thing. But I need parts for all the guys in the band.'

Bobby said: 'I'll play the record to them as well!'

'I'm sorry,' said Bob Miller. 'They need to read the music. They want parts.'

'Well, where am I supposed to get parts?' Bobby almost shouted at him.

'Ring the publisher,' he suggested.

The publisher was Dick James, a friend of ours. Bobby said to him: 'I'm with Bob Miller at the BBC, and he says he wants parts for his band!'

Dick said: 'Well, haven't you got them?'

'No, I haven't!' yelled Bobby.

'Oh dear,' said Dick, or words to that effect, and he arranged for a set to be photocopied and rushed over to the Playhouse in Charing Cross, where we were doing the broadcast. And that is how I learned that I needed band parts for my songs.

When I went to the Palladium in 1964 I was extra well prepared – or I thought I was. *Anyone Who Had A Heart* had just been released, and we went into the theatre with the recording scores for that song and for *You're My World*. What neither Bobby nor I realized was that recording scores are in the highest possible key, and what you don't want to have to do twice nightly and three times on Saturday is to sing in the highest possible key. For the sake of your voice you take it down half a tone. But I didn't know that – and lost my voice and had to miss a couple of shows.

It was the local MD (musical director) who spotted what was wrong. He was furious that no-one had advised us about this before, and in fact he took the keys down for us.

✳✳✳✳

There was another main reason why it took time to adjust to life in show business. A lot of musicians from Liverpool had this problem, but it was probably more difficult for a solo performer like me. Just as Liverpudlians are a race apart, so the music we liked took a different direction from the rest of the country. Everywhere else people were overawed by what happened in London. In Liverpool we had our own versions of everything, and no-one for a minute thought they were inferior.

London had its Soho clubs like the 2 Is; all right, we had the Cavern, the Iron Door, etc. We had our own music paper, *Merseybeat*, which was started by Bill Harry, and we had our own hit parade based on what was selling in Liverpool shops. Others might say we were out of step, but we were happy the way we were, and anyone else could lump it.

What happened in the early Sixties in Liverpool was a rebellion. We did it through music, whereas today they use violence, but the causes weren't that different. For years we had been dominated by outsiders. Every day visitors came in through the port of Liverpool and told us what a load of rubbish we were, how filthy and decrepit the city was. No cures were offered, but everyone we met seemed to be totally under the influence of American culture. We lived in a world where the model of all that was good in life was a Doris Day movie. In Liverpool itself I'd see older girls sitting on the steps of tenements making themselves up and talking excitedly of Burtonwood – the American base they all went to for their taste of honey.

In music we were also dominated by Americans, but in our case it wasn't the white college sound we listened to but the blues of the black people. It may have been music for underdogs but we thought it was beautiful. Dinah Washington I loved, and the R & B singers like Bo Did-dley, Little Richard, The Platters – those were the people who influenced me, and they had the same effect on The Beatles. We all loved Elvis as well, and Jerry Lee Lewis, but it was the black groups like The Miracles who showed us the way.

So we carried on with our own brand of separate development, up to the stage where we began to get dates to appear outside Liverpool. When this happened, the outside world was a revelation. I'd only been to Chester before, and now we were off on tour to Sheffield! All my life I had been totally focussed on Liverpool, which I assumed was unique. Now I was amazed to find that Sheffield also had a Marks and Spencer, and a Woolies, and you could buy Coca Cola there!

Then came London, a completely foreign place where I was to spend two homesick years. If I was starting in the business today, there is no way I would leave Liverpool. I went through a lot of misery trying to get used to London and its very different culture. I missed my friends, my family, the cooking, everything. For nine months of that time I was at the London Palla-dium, and it was that long booking which got me used to London. I lived in a hotel for two years, not buying a place of my own because I didn't want to break the bond with Liverpool which I still thought of as my home.

A lot of people couldn't understand it. They thought I'd love living in London – and perhaps I might have, if I'd got to know one of the residen-tial parts. But the London that I knew was the West End – theatreland – full of tourists and foreigners, a place where nobody lived. Then I met Cathy

McGowan who did the *Ready Steady Go* programmes, and became very friendly with her. She took me to her home in Streatham, and that was a revelation because it was so much more like Liverpool. 'Oh,' I thought. 'London isn't all that different after all.'

In a way it was still more unsettling to find out about somewhere like Streatham after I had been plonked down in the middle of town. I was still only twenty years old, and up till then I'd had a very close-knit family life.

Even the people I worked with were very different. Where I was used to appearing on rock and roll bills with bands like The Beatles, Gerry and the Pacemakers and a bunch of other, mainly Liverpool groups, as soon as I had a hit record I was whisked away and put on a bill on my own with a load of acts beneath me that I'd mostly never heard of, and sent off to do rock and roll tours. On the touring circuit I worked with some big names like the Everley Brothers and P.J. Proby, and they were nice people – but it was still a lonely life. Even though Bobby was with me, as my personal manager, he too was going through the same learning process and finding it all as strange as I did.

In those first months I learnt a lot about travelling from one date to another. It was the age of the coach, when everyone went by coach including the star. Later we had Americans coming over who refused to go on a coach and insisted on having their own limo – and as a result of that everyone wanted a limo. But the old days of the coach were great fun; we had lots of laughs. It never seemed to matter where we were going, we always stopped off at Grantham, near the A1. We stopped there for lunch a lot of the time, and I learned to eat very fast. If you didn't get your meal down quick, the coach would be off without you!

In Dublin I came downstairs in the hotel one Sunday morning, ready to catch the coach to Belfast, and the hall porter told me I was too late, it had gone. I wasn't very pleased about this because I wasn't late at all. Still, if the bus had gone, it had gone. I had to trail down to the station and catch a train. In Belfast I still reached the venue half an hour before the others.

'What did you think you were doing,' I yelled at them, 'leaving Dublin without me?'

It turned out they hadn't left at all. While I was heading for the station, cursing them under my breath, they were still in bed snoring their heads off. The real idiot was the hotel porter, who gave me a complete load of rubbish.

At the Palladium I had a more regular life, working on a traditional variety bill with Frankie Vaughan and Tommy Cooper, plus the Fourmost to add a little bit of Liverpool. On Saturdays I'd go in there at eleven in the morning, do three shows and finish at eleven o'clock at night. Then Bobby drove me straight home to Liverpool so I could have Sunday lunch with the

In no time at all I went from being Priscilla White of the typing pool – but don't ask me why I'm picking my teeth with a ruler – to working with incredible people like Burt Bacharach (at the piano) and George Martin, my recording manager. It's hardly surprising that there were a few gaps in what I knew about music, or singing, or the world outside Liverpool – in fact, you name it, I didn't know about it!

It was fantastic when so many people from Liverpool – like Jimmy Tarbuck and Gerry Marsden, not to mention The Beatles – hit the front at the same time, because we could all share the novelty together. Then, less than a year after my first record came out, I was at the Palladium with two of the biggest names in British show business – Tommy Cooper and Frankie Vaughan. This picture was taken on my twenty-first birthday.

By 1965 British bands and singers were riding on an amazing wave of popularity. See how many faces you can recognize from the performers and presenters at this Wembley concert.

family. Most of the route was by the old A-roads and it took five to six hours.

My family were always pleased to see me, but they never let my comings and goings interfere with their own routines. If one of them had to go out, they went – never mind the fact that their daughter (the Celebrity) had just driven up from London to see them. One Sunday I was left there with only Lassie the dog to talk to! At least there was no danger of getting big-headed in my family.

When you are young and naive, you need a few bumps to teach you what it's all about. I learnt much of my craft at the Palladium – and that included being fined for missing finales. It was arrogant of me really, but I didn't like going to finales, or, as we call them in the business, 'Who's best'. I didn't see the point of putting on a different frock and walking down a load of steps when I'd already been on and done my act, so for a while I didn't take them seriously.

I'd be in my dressing room when they came round with the ten-minute call, but then I'd somehow let it slip my mind. I'd be so engrossed in washing a pair of tights that the time would whizz by – until suddenly it was too late and I'd missed the finale. The management didn't like it one bit; as far as they were concerned, finales were an important part of the show and it was traditional that you turned up for them. To make the point, Jack Matthews, the stage manager, threatened a small fine. That soon cured me.

Slowly I began to learn that I had a responsibility towards the audience – the paying public. Instead of taking it for granted that every house would be packed to the roof with cheering fans, I started to distinguish between one audience and another, and to ask what they were like before I went on. Gradually I learned professional habits, like how to move onstage with presence, and make a good entrance. But these were all things that took time. In 1963-64 my world was turning very fast, and it's hardly surprising I didn't learn everything overnight – or in the right order.

I was plugging *Love of the Loved* on Southern Television. Bobby was with me and he asked the director what I should do during an eight-bar instrumental break.

'Oh,' he said, 'just dance around. Anything you like. We'll follow you.'

It was a live programme, and when the instrumental break came up I danced right past the camera and out of sight, then danced back on to the set.

Up in the gallery, where Bobby was sitting, the TV people couldn't believe it.

'What's that she's doing now?' they asked in amazement.

Bobby defended me. 'You said she could dance anywhere,' he said.

'Yes,' they said, as if talking to a child of five. 'Anywhere-in-front-of-the-camera, lovey.'

Some people who saw me do that programme thought I had danced off the set deliberately, as if it had something to do with my Liverpool sense of humour. But really there was a much simpler reason: I was just being thick, that's all.

A R E   Y O U
A N Y B O D Y ?

*'When I first came to London and stayed in a hotel
there was a phone beside the bed. I thought: "Wow!
This is the greatest thing." I was going to call everyone
I knew. Then I realized that everyone under the sun
I knew didn't have a phone.'*

That upset me quite a lot – to think that I had made it but I couldn't tell anyone about it. And yet, although it was a big jump from my very modest Liverpool background, I took to luxury and the star treatment quite easily. Partly this was because I had spent a large part of my childhood and teens in a dream world ruled by the magic of Hollywood.

In any movie starring Doris Day, or Debbie Reynolds or Natalie Wood, you never saw the sordid side of life, it was all a wonderful candyfloss dream played in a glamorous show

24

business setting, or on a university campus where all the students were at- tractive and well dressed, and went to beautiful gleaming drugstores and had homes with luxury furniture and amazing kitchens. I suppose it was sheer propaganda for the American way of life, but it could look very al- luring when the home you went back to after the cinema was over a bar- ber's shop and next to a Chinese laundry in the Scotland Road. Number 380. Not long ago they offered us the sign from the barber's shop. I wish we'd taken it, but we never got beyond the stage of wondering how you got an eight-foot sign from Liverpool to Buckinghamshire.

Outside my own dream world I had precious little contact with luxury. It was a big event, for instance, when the Chinese laundry's water supply broke down and I filled and carried buckets into the laundry so they could keep up with the washing. In return they gave me a Cadbury's Flake, which was my idea of heaven. I would do anything for a Cadbury's Flake (and still do today!).

All that time I never had any doubt that I would become a star. From the age of about eleven I was coming into the house and announcing: 'Next week I am going to be a star,' and no-one ever discouraged me. So really it was more a matter of waiting until it happened, rather than just hoping. I was always confident that I had a talent, and that one day it would be recognized. It may have been naive to think that way, but that's how I was.

Not all the changes in my life met with the approval of me Dad. Although he was generally happy for me, he didn't approve of the change of name from White to Black, which began as a misprint in *Merseybeat*. Brian Epstein saw it, liked it, and when the time came for me to sign with him, I was 'Cilla Black' on the management contract which me Dad had to sign because I was under twenty-one.

'What's this?' Dad wanted to know when Brian came to our house with the papers. 'Why Cilla Black? Her name's White.'

Brian, who was really a very shy person, had some trouble explain- ing that when he first saw my name in *Merseybeat,* he didn't know it was a misprint, and by the time he found out he thought Black was a better name for a singer. To me it didn't seem that important because I was known around Liverpool as Cilla, or Swinging Cilla, or Swinging Priscilla, and the surname didn't really enter into it. But to me Dad it seemed an unnecessary change. At the back of his mind was the idea that the family would lose out if I stopped being Cilla White. Down on the docks where he worked his mates would never believe him if he pointed to my name in the paper and said: 'Cilla Black. That's my daughter.' 'Oh yes,' they'd say. 'Pull the other one.'

So when Brian came to the house he had to be firm, despite his embarrassment. 'I rather like it' was the line he took, and in the end Dad signed.

Other would-be managers had made the trip to our house for Sunday tea and an interview with me Dad. We called them 'the Cockney fellers', and they'd been coming round since I was sixteen. On Sundays me Dad went to the pub at noon, came home for his dinner, had an hour upstairs in bed and then came down for tea. 'Ey, Dad,' I'd say, pointing to some feller in a suit, 'he wants to be my manager.'

'No,' Dad would say later, 'I didn't like the look of that one,' or 'No, he speaks funny.'

Brian was the only one who made a good personal impression. Also there was the fact that he was local, and that his family owned the furniture store – Epsteins – from which we had bought a piano. Obviously he came from a family which had more than two ha'pennies to rub to- gether, and I'm sure this influenced me Dad.

After he'd signed, Dad may have worried that he was losing a daughter, almost as if my new name meant I was getting married to show business as well as leaving home for London, but he never let me forget that he was still my father and that he hadn't signed away his authority over me. One weekend, a few weeks later, I arrived back home from Lon- don and sat down in his favourite armchair. When Dad came in, it was the first thing he noticed, and he told me in no uncertain terms to get out of *his*chair, who did I think I was, etcetera. Some changes he might accept, but that was far too close to Home.

In the coming months I learned a lot about the way success means you have to adapt your lifestyle. Girl singers didn't get the same physical hassle as the boys, but I still got a huge amount of attention from fans and autograph hunters, especially as I was the only girl to come out of the Liverpool Explosion. Anyone in our group would be fair game, and kids would rush up to Bobby waving their books and pens and shouting: 'Are you anybody?'

Bobby's answer was always no, but that still didn't save him the day we left the studios of Southern Television after a broadcast. Suddenly he was attacked by a mob of teenage girls who grabbed him and pulled him over and started wrestling with him on the ground. They were like a lot of wild animals, completely hysterical – and Bobby had only left the building first in order to pave the way for me!

I followed him out, and that day the fact that I was a girl counted for nothing. They rushed at me, grabbing and clawing like vultures. I was wear- ing a black plastic mac by Mary Quant which I was very proud of and which

With Brian Epstein. He was the most marvellous manager and friend, and gave me the confidence to do things that I would never have dared to take on without him in the background.

Outside Broadcasting House with the Bentley – what Brian called 'a Princess of the Road for the Queen of Pop.'

One of my best London friends was Cathy McGowan, of Ready Steady Go! *She introduced me to her home district, Streatham, and told me where to shop in London for clothes. In this picture she and I are helping the staff of Biba on the day they moved into their new place in Kensington Church Street.*

In 1967 The Beatles threw a famous fancy-dress party for the Magical Mystery Tour. I went as Charlie Chaplin (that's the actor George Playdon next to me in the interesting bra) and Bobby went as a nun (that's Peter Brown, Brian Epstein's assistant, with a hand up his robe).

The Italian waiters were most distressed when this nun kept coming up to them blowing smoke all over the place and asking for whisky and Cokes. Going to the party, we had a hysterial drive because Bobby was at the wheel and all over the West End heads were swivelling at the sight of a nun driving a Rolls-Royce. But he does look all cherubic, doesn't he? At the party, when he lined up for a conga, a feller stepped back and said to him: 'After you, love.'

This is when we went to Jimmy Tarbuck's birthday party. He'd hired a discotheque and Bobby went as a brain surgeon. While we were in there, someone broke into one of the guests' cars in the car park and the police were called. Unfortunately, they didn't go away but hung around outside. When we left, one of them followed us and Bobby got breathalyzed. It was bad luck on him because he'd been on a diet and at the party he had hardly drunk anything all evening. Just towards the end, the fish and chips arrived and he thought: 'I'll have a glass of wine with those.' So he'd had a couple of glasses of champagne to wash down the fish and chips and toast Jimmy's birthday, and then we left. When the police stopped us, Bobby was just over the limit and they wanted me to take the keys and drive home, not realizing that I'd been drinking white wine at the party and was well ahead of Bobby! I said no, I couldn't drive, and so did Bobby! An hour later, he blew into the bag and was clear, so he drove us home. It still cost him his licence for a year, so now he's given up brain surgery.

had cost a fortune. In seconds it was destroyed – buttons ripped off, the bottom of it in shreds. It really upset me, because you can't repair plastic, and here was a new designer coat which so-called fans had ripped to pieces in about five seconds.

In the previous chapter I mentioned having a bad throat and having to miss some shows at the Palladium. Naturally I went back to Liverpool, which I still felt was my proper home, to have a short rest and get some sea air. I looked forward to going cockling at Moreton with Bobby, and to spending time on the beach at New Brighton, just like we used to do. But it was impossible. Everywhere we went we were swamped by people wanting autographs. I couldn't understand what all the fuss was about, but it never went away the whole time we were up there.

The strange thing was, I could hide away much better in the West End of London. In Oxford Street or Leicester Square people still came up to me, but mostly it was just to say hello – whereas in Liverpool I stuck out like a sore thumb.

Bobby and I went to a late movie in Leicester Square one night after I'd finished my show at the Palladium. In 1964 I still thought I could go anywhere, so if I wanted to go to the pictures I'd just turn up and queue with everyone else. Fortunately, on that particular evening there weren't many people around; I did a few autographs and then we went in and sat down. I think I'll let Bobby tell the rest of this story.

Bobby: 'We hadn't been watching the film long when Cilla began to nod off. I waited till she was asleep, then crept out and went and sat about four rows behind her. When the lights came up, a feller in the same row saw who she was; he was across with the pen and paper before Cilla had woken up properly. He was saying: 'Can I have your autograph' while she was still wondering, first of all, where she was, then where I'd got to – and then what was she doing waking up with a strange feller!'

At night, after a Palladium show, we hadn't a clue what to do with ourselves. We didn't know any clubs or restaurants, so we were just as likely to finish up at the Golden Egg in Leicester Square, sitting under the bright lights while everyone stared at us. I suppose I had always assumed that if I became successful it would be like winning the pools and that the magic 'they' would take care of everything. 'They' would tell you where to eat, 'they' would say which shops to go to, 'they' would recommend a place to have your hair done. In fact it wasn't like that at all. When work was over for the night, everyone else went off and lived their own life. There was no magic 'they' – it was you yourself who had to do it.

To some extent Brian Epstein helped us – when he was able to. He had terrific style, and his early background meant he automatically knew things that were completely foreign to us. He'd had a great schooling, he came from a posh family, and he had money. He was marvellous for us, and I adored him. Perhaps his own background led him to assume that, on the social side, we knew more about the big wide world than we really did. But it was anyway not in his nature to interfere. At the same time, he too was a learner. He had to teach himself about music and orchestration and all the technical side of the business, quite apart from turning himself into a successful show business agent.

What Brian achieved for all the people he managed was amazing. In those days the big agents were Lew and Leslie Grade and their brother, Bernard Delfont. Brian, when he began, was just a young Northern executive trying to make a go of it in show business. You'd think he might have found it daunting to break into the London scene. Most out-of-town agents would have been more cautious, maybe gone in with the Grades while they found their feet. Not Brian. He went straight in and set up his own London office.

It was not only a bold move, it was incredibly successful – as everyone now should know. For all of us who were on the inside, a special bond was formed between us. Whether it was the girl who did the typing or one of the performers, there was a great sense of pride in what we were all doing – *together*. In a way it was Liverpool versus The Rest, so if anyone – me, The Beatles, Billy J. Kramer and The Dakotas, Gerry and The Pacemakers – had a hit record, everyone shared in the triumph.

Part of the celebrations involved buying ourselves nice big cars – but here I wasn't too clever. When *Anyone Who Had a Heart* was No 1, I ordered myself a Jaguar. Then I started to look round and I noticed that the fellers were busy getting themselves Rolls Royces. I went to see Brian.

'Ey, Brian,' I said, 'how come – with my record selling a hundred thousand copies a day – I can't have a Rolls Royce as well.'

Brian said: 'There's no reason at all why you shouldn't.' Then he showed an extra bit of class. 'But really you should have a Bentley,' he went on. 'A Princess of the Road for the Queen of Pop.'

The Jaguar never left the showroom, and I lost £75 on the trade-in, which in those days was an awful lot of money. But it was worth it, just, to own what I thought was the dream car to end them all.

We were a family, and when Brian died it was tragic for all of us. It happened in 1967, when I was on holiday in Portugal with Bobby and some friends, including Tom Jones. He and I had become good friends ever since he joined me on tour to fill in for P.J. Proby – Old Splitting Pants – who had got

31

a bit outrageous and been dropped from the tour. We were all in this club one Sunday night when the waiter came over.

He said: 'Are you Cilla Black?'

I said I was.

'Your manager's dead.'

I couldn't believe what I'd just heard. I thought it was some kind of sick joke. I looked at Bobby, and he was all for putting one on the waiter there and then. He was furious. Then Tom had the idea of phoning the local paper to see if they had any news. At first we only got garbled messages – yes, he'd shot himself, he'd done this, he'd done that. Although the Algarve is only a couple of hours from London, we felt completely isolated and just sat around in shock until we could get a proper account of what had happened.

The strange thing was, that weekend no-one close to Brian was in London. The Beatles were in Bangor with the Maharishi; Gerry Marsden was at his place in Wales; we were in Portugal; Brian's mother was in Liverpool; Peter Brown was in Sussex; Vivienne Moynahan, a friend he often phoned, was working in Russia. Had Brian wanted to get in touch, he'd have had little or no luck at all. It was pure coincidence, but almost uncanny the way his friends were suddenly not there when he was going through this terrible, fatal crisis.

There is no doubt that Brian had a deeply unhappy private life. But, whatever others may say or write, I will always think of him as I knew him. He was wonderful to me, always caring and protective. To him I was 'My Cilla'. When I went with him to a premiere, he made me feel like a million dollars – me from the poor background with nothing to my name, he with everything a girl would wish for. It was a tragic waste that he should die so young. If only he had talked more to his friends, opened up a little so we could have shared the pressures that were getting him down. But it was not to be.

****

Back in 1964, I was still the naive beginner trying to adjust to the strange business of being 'somebody'. As I said earlier, I soon found that there was no magic 'they' to put me on the right track, but I did meet some kind people who helped me a lot.

On the fashion side, Cathy McGowan told me about Biba, which was just opening. John Lyndon was another good friend who taught me a lot. He was a producer for NEMS, brought in by Brian Epstein, and he taught me about food and wine, and also about art. He had a most marvellous collection of theatre posters which he picked up at markets like the Portobello Road,

*On our wedding day
in London, at
Marylebone Register
Office on the 25th
January 1969. In
the background is
Peter Brown. At the
celebrations later on,
Bobby is hanging on
to me and Judy
Martin. In front is
Gabrielle Crawford,
wife of Michael
Crawford, and the
two other fellers are
Peter Brown and
Tommy Nutter.*

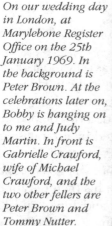

*Here I am (below) in 1970,
receiving my first* Sun
*award for Top Female
Television Personality from
Harold Wilson, then prime
minister. A few days earlier,
Mr Wilson had asked a
group of show-business
people to tea at Number 10,
but I hadn't been invited.
Me Dad was quite upset
about this, and as a good
Socialist docker he wanted
to know why. I told him I'd
be seeing the prime minister
soon, and I'd ask him.
When I did, he just gave me
one of those politician's
smiles and didn't say
anything. I never did get to
Number 10 while he
was in office, but later
Mr Callaghan asked
me so I don't feel I've
been totally forgotten
by the Government.*

and when Bobby and I began to collect paintings he advised us about what to buy and what to leave alone.

When it came to deciding on a painting, I was only too happy to have someone else offer their guidance, but no art expert in the world would have persuaded me to buy any of a set of very tasteful pictures that were brought round to the office one day. They all showed nude boys draped around a swimming pool, and the fact that they were painted by a promising young artist called David Hockney made no impression on me at all. The only thing I could think was: 'If I put that on our wall, me Mum will go *ber-serk!*'

John Lyndon is now doing very well with his own restaurant near Lewes in Sussex. He put us right about things to eat and drink – and it's just as well he did because in those days we were still having conversations like this:

Bobby, to Dionne Warwick who had just arrived in our dressing room: 'What would you like to drink?'

Dionne Warwick: 'I'll have a Cognac, please.'

Bobby: 'I'm sorry, we've only got brandy.'

We didn't know anything about drink because in Liverpool no-one kept drink in the house. If you did, then it was a safe bet you were having either a funeral or a wedding. The rest of the time, the kettle was on the hob and you could have tea till it came out your ears, but nothing alcoholic. If the men wanted a drink, they went down the pub. And when Bobby and I came down to London, we never had wine with our meal. In restaurants we'd order steak and chips and Coca Cola. The first person to introduce us to wine was Muriel Young, a television presenter and good friend, who recommended we try Mateus Rose.

The funny thing about Mateus was that it became a kind of cult drink with the rock bands. The Stones were on Mateus, for instance. You'd see them come into a club, and they'd all order it. 'Mateus, please.' 'Yeah, I'll have a Mateus.' 'Same for me.' 'Yeah.' 'Yeah.' Suddenly the clubs were doing a roaring trade in pink Portuguese wine.

Muriel tells a great story about when she was Auntie Mu on the *Five O'Clock Show*. With her as guests one day she had two puppets, Olly Beak the Owl and Fred the Dog (who is now Basil Brush). They were getting close to the end of the show, but then Mu saw the floor manager signalling that she was under-time, so she had to carry on talking.

Well, that's alright with humans, but how do you fill in for two or three long minutes when you've only got puppets to chat to? Mu gave it her best. She turned to Olly Beak and said:

'Olly, what have you been doing with yourself lately?'

'Well,' said Olly, 'it's been lovely.The other day I was invited to a ball.'

34

Muriel looked at him sternly: 'Don't be silly, Olly,' she said. 'Owls don't have balls!'

Olly Beak and Fred the Dog shrank quickly out of view – and Auntie Mu was left to finish the programme by herself! Happily, it didn't finish her career, because she went on to become a very successful producer.

It was Muriel who put us on to the Pickwick Club, a marvellous place just off Leicester Square, and we went there quite a lot during our Mateus Period. Then I heard Brian Epstein talking to someone about the Ad-Lib. I asked him what it was.

'It's a club,' he said. 'But I'm not going to take you, because if I take you there you'll never be out of it.'

'Oh please take me,' I begged him. So in the end he did – and he was quite right. It was the most wonderful place where the people from the bands could go and not be stared at. Because so many of our friends started going there it was like being back at The Cavern – even if it was a trillion times more expensive. The cult drink, meanwhile, had moved on from Mateus and became whisky and Coke. Then The Beatles came back from New York with a different message.

'You don't want that,' they said, when whisky and Coke was mentioned. 'You want bourbon and 7-Up.'

So everyone switched to that. Not that I ever drank much of it. I never have liked spirits much, and the price the Ad-Lib charged for a bourbon and 7-Up made sure I nursed one glass the whole night.

If there is one thing I regret about those club nights, it was that we never offered to pay the bill when Mu Young took us out. She was often ringing us up and taking us down to the Pickwick or out to a restaurant, but somehow it never dawned on us to pay. All I can say is that we had a lot to learn in those days and it was bound to take a little time before we came through.

I was never intimidated by anyone, no matter how grand they were – even royalty. That must have come from something natural in me, and I am very grateful for it. But I did also get a lot of encouragement from good friends, especially from Brian who used to point me in a particular direction and tell me that, whatever it was, I could do it.

He was probably the greatest source of my confidence. He told me I could do virtually anything. So I did it!

LADY ON
THE ROCKS

'I go cold to think about some of the things I've done in films and to publicize songs. I'm sure that if they'd put half the things on paper and said: "This is what you're going to do," I'd never have said yes.'

When *You're My World* reached No 1, they had me standing on a wall on the roof of a big hotel. All London was beneath me. It made a lovely picture, except that I didn't have anything between me and 'all London'.

'Just step up there,' they said, 'face the cameras and throw your arms out.'

So I did. When you're that age – I was twenty-one – you don't stop to weigh up all the dangers, you act much more spontaneously. There was something else as well. Brian Epstein persuaded me, very early on, that if I had faith in

other people, I would be able to do things that otherwise I'd never dream of doing. So if, for instance, my television producer said: 'It's all right, there's no danger,' I'd jump out of a helicopter.

I did that as well – and not so very long ago. It was for a *Surprise Surprise* feature on the Air-Sea Rescue service. We told them that we wanted to know what it was like to be saved by one of their rescue helicopters. What we didn't tell them was that when they came on the show to see our film of the rescue, we were going to surprise them by bringing on fifty people they had rescued.

In order to be saved on television, first I had to be 'lost'. I put on the flying suit, plus a pair of earphones which gave some protection against the terrible noise and a microphone to catch my every reaction, and we took off. So far so good – well, apart from the briefing.

Before we went out to the helicopter, I had to have a half-hour briefing to learn about all the safety measures and what to do in an emergency. I wouldn't mind, but there are so many things you have to remember – like if the helicopter goes into the sea, you're supposed to try and climb out of one particular window. As the briefing went on I grew more and more nervous, because I was looking around the room and thinking: 'It's all right for them, they know all this stuff. But I haven't a clue – and I've forgotten half of what he's said so far!'

All too soon we were hovering above the rock where I was to be marooned. It was all isolated and spiky-looking, not flat on top like they'd said it would be. Over by the cliffs I could see the second camera crew who would be filming the rescue from a distance; I knew Bobby would be with them.

'What you have to do,' said my instructor, 'is follow me out of the helicopter. I'll be on the line just below the door, and then you sit on the edge with your legs over the side. When my colleague gives the word, you jump out and put your legs round my waist and just hold on. Then we'll winch you down to the rock and leave you there for a few minutes before we come and do the rescue.'

It was definitely one of those times to have faith in others. At least, with all the gear surrounding you, and the noise of the helicopter, you don't have much time for private thought. When the moment came, I jumped, and instantly the world was a different place as I hung there in space and then was winched down to the rock.

It wasn't what you'd call a comfortable rock. It was all pointy, with no proper place to stand or sit, but I found myself a niche and got in there and waited.

Another thing they didn't tell me was that they'd be away for some time. First, as I found out later, they had to go off and refuel, and then they had to get their camera set up to film the rescue. Only after all that had been done would they come back to the rock. To kill time, and stop myself thinking too much, I got my make-up out and started powdering my nose. I was talking to myself as well, forgetting I was miked up, so that people miles away could hear me muttering things like: 'Is it really true what Bobby said, about the rock being completely covered at high water? No, it can't be, it's much too tall. If you look down from here – no, better not look down . . . Where *are* they?'

Well, they did turn up in the end. I wasn't submerged by the tide, the rescue was filmed, and we all got back to base. But if you ask me if I enjoyed it, I'm afraid the answer is no. I did find it disturbing, however much faith I may have had in the ability of those Air-Sea Rescue fellers to drive a helicopter and winch people in and out of it. When we arrived back on dry land, the first thing I did was go down on my knees and kiss the ground.

✳✳✳✳

I made a film which Sir Peter Hall directed, called *Work Is A Four Letter Word*. I was also appearing every evening in *Way Out In Piccadilly* with Frankie Howerd. This meant getting home at midnight after the second show, going straight to bed and then getting up at four o'clock in the morning and driving up to Birmingham to do location work on the film.

It was a very Sixties/early Seventies type of fantasy film, and in one of the scenes I was captured by a mad earth-moving machine which had a mind of its own. In the script I had just eaten a magic mushroom and gone to sleep on the grass – when along came this digger.

In the script it came up alongside me, thumped its bucket down on the ground, I fell into the bucket and was carried off. To give them their due, they did rehearse the scene several times, using a cross on the ground for the digger to aim at. It always missed its mark, but they must have decided it was near enough so they went ahead and filmed the scene. I did one take and then Bobby, who was in more of a panic than me, said he was very sorry but that was all I was doing. Finish. No more takes with the digger. So we moved on to the scene with the crane.

I don't know which was worse. If you were me, would you rather risk being bonged on the head by the bucket of a not-very-accurate mechanical digger or be whisked by crane seventy feet up in the air on a metal hook, with nothing to hold on to but the chain? Not an easy choice.

39

I felt fine, or fairly fine, going up through the air. It was when the crane driver put on the brake and the hook, which was shaped like an anchor, started swinging from side to side – that was when the waves of panic started rising. I didn't actually go all weak, but I was certainly thinking: 'What happens if I do go all weak?'

In their enthusiasm to film the scene, no-one had thought of rigging some kind of harness to the chain, so that if I slipped I would at least be saved from the big drop. Now I was swaying about, sat on one side of this anchor, praying. Next to me was a tall building, and there at a window was one of the stunt men. He looked at me, and I looked at him, and he understood.

'Get her down!' he started shouting. 'Get her down.'

As luck would have it, no-one argued. Down I went on the anchor, until I was safely on the ground. This time the stunt man made sure I had a proper harness, and we shot the scene again.

In a way, it wasn't all that surprising to find myself doing things which were beyond the call of duty. Sir Peter Hall is renowned in the acting business for wanting to get as much realism into his plays as possible. In one of his stage productions there was a guillotine, and the actor due to be executed was, understandably, a little worried. He was worried because the prop was a *real* guillotine, and he was being asked to put his head on the block, as though for real. In the play itself, when the word was given, the knife would actually fall and the only thing to prevent them needing a new actor each night was a set of bolts fixed in the sides of the frame which stopped the blade about a quarter of an inch above the actor's neck.

They could have used a papier-mâché substitute, but Sir Peter wanted the sound of a metal blade hissing down and Thunk! The actor wanted no part of it. In rehearsals they demonstrated the guillotine several times, and each time it did exactly what it was meant to – the blade whistled down and was stopped by the bolts. Still the actor wouldn't do it.

'Look,' said Sir Peter, 'I'll show you. I'll do it myself. Watch this.'

He put his head under the knife. Down it came – Whack! The bolts stopped it, and Sir Peter withdrew his head. So now the actor felt a little bit less lonely, and after a bit more persuading he agreed to do it.

'But before I get under there,' he said, 'just let me see what happens once more.'

So they raised the knife to the top of the guillotine, and brought it down again. It came slashing through the air, sheered through the bolts and smashed into the block. If there'd been a head in the way, it would have jumped straight in the basket.

I'd rather not think about it any more.

All set for a ride in the Navy Rescue helicopter. Don't I look cheerful!

In the bucket of the giant digger with David Warner, while filming Work Is A Four Letter Word.

In the same series as the Air-Sea Rescue feature, I had a meeting to remember with an alligator. As you might expect, I sang to it – and you can probably guess which song it was – but the main event was when I went into its cage and scrubbed its teeth.

'Don't worry,' they said, 'it'll be fine.' (They must have heard about my need to have faith in the people I work with, because now they were extending it to wild animals!) 'It'll be quite all right because by the time you go in there it won't have had any heat for twenty-four hours, and that always makes alligators sleepy.'

I had never thought much about it before, but apparently alligators in captivity have to have their teeth cleaned once a week. In the wild, they have ticks and small birds who go in there and pick out all the bits of rubbish for them, but in zoos and safari parks in this country they need keepers and people like me to do it for them.

I went down to Poole in Dorset and met up with everyone involved. The camera crew had been there since seven o'clock in the morning, and one disconcerting thing I noticed early on was that the alligators and crocodiles in this enclosure weren't looking docile or dozy at all. Probably it was the heat of the camera lights which had stirred them, but to me they looked quite frisky.

Doing this little film with the alligator must have been on my mind for a while, because I remember taking off my ring before I went into the cage. I said to myself: 'I can put up with losing a finger, but I *don't* want to lose my ring.'

So in I went. Most of the camera crew stayed outside, but one feller came in with me, and the alligator's handler was there as well. We didn't just walk in through a gate, that would have been too easy. We had to crawl through a tunnel at the back until we came to the place where the alligator was, well, not exactly waiting for us, but it didn't seem all that surprised either.

I began with a song, *See You Later Alligator* (did you guess?), and scrubbed its back with a scrubbing brush. It lay quite still and let me, so that was fine. Then came the *piéce de résistance,* where I cleaned its teeth. They passed me what looked like a huge toothbrush, and I went up to it again. By then it was hissing a bit which, I later found out, means they aren't very happy. The alligator took one look at me, its jaws came open and – Crack! It snapped the toothbrush clean in two.

Two things occurred to me around this time. One was that the only protection we had in that enclosure was the keeper's broom. The other was that I didn't like it in there; more to the point, I wanted to get out – and fast!

Actually, I surprised myself by not going into a total panic and screaming the place down. Instead, with a presence of mind that must have been born of pure terror, I turned to the camera and said:

'I don't like this. I would like to get out of here.'

Slowly I edged towards the exit tunnel and crawled out to safety, past a row of what I thought were logs, or stuffed animals, but which were actually small crocodiles.

I go quite cold to think about it now. Even the hook or the helicopter seem like nice little jobs compared with my time in the alligator's den.

When I did my first *Disneytime* for BBC television, I was in a summer season at Blackpool. I met the people to discuss the show and someone said:

'Wouldn't it be nice if we could do the show with animals. Each time you introduce a cartoon, you're with a different animal.'

'Fine,' I said.

Various animals were mentioned – horses, dolphins, a parrot, a snake, a monkey . . . I didn't mind appearing with any of the tamed animals, because they had their handlers with them. Feeding the dolphins, for instance, was lovely. No, the only animal I was unhappy about was the parrot. Bobby had found it in a pet shop in Blackpool, together with the monkey, and on the day we did the recording in a local park, there it was.

'Now, Cilla,' said the director, 'put the parrot on your shoulder and we'll link into the next cartoon.'

I said: 'I don't really want to do that.'

'What on earth do you mean?' asked the director.

It was difficult to explain. Maybe it was a general feeling of uneasiness which I had about *all* parrots, not just this one. All I could say was: 'I don't know. I don't fancy it, that's all.'

The director was getting impatient. 'Look,' he said, 'what is the matter with you?'

'I don't know,' I said miserably. 'I don't like the look of its beak. I don't fancy that beak sitting on my shoulder.'

In the end Bobby said he'd show me how to do it. The parrot was brought over, placed on Bobby's shoulder, and immediately sank its beak into his neck and hung on.

'Right,' I said. 'You can forget me doing that.'

So they put the parrot – once they'd prised it off Bobby – in a tree and we did the scene with the two of us kept well apart.

Later I had reservations about filming with the monkey which had come from the same shop. Quite right too – it bit the stand-in's leg! Bobby was more disappointed than angry. He said the animals had been fine and well-behaved in the shop. He'd been going in there regularly to buy meat for our dogs and he'd seen them on several occasions, being stroked by children and generally giving no problems at all. Once out of the shop, however, the environment they'd grown used to, they turned a bit snappy. Not unlike the chimpanzees in New York.

The first time I appeared on the *Ed Sullivan Show,* I followed a chimpanzee act. All day in rehearsals I had been going on after these chimpanzees and they were very good. They had a circus ring and they rode motor-bikes round it and performed amazing tricks.

Then, during a break, the producers of the show decided that the circus ring was too big because their cameras couldn't get the variety of shots they wanted. So they took out some of the sections and made the circuit shorter. Fine – except the chimps didn't know it was shorter. They'd only been trained in the full-sized ring. The trainer could have said something, but I expect he was terrified of being thrown off the *Ed Sullivan Show* if he complained. It was the most popular TV show in the United States, and also had a reputation for ruthlessness. It didn't matter who you were, or how far you'd come to do the show, if they didn't like you on the run-through you were out.

So on came the chimps to do the live show, and straight away it turned into chaos. The chimps couldn't cope with the smaller ring, which threw out all their moves. Soon they were going every which-way, and getting very cross each time they crashed into each other instead of narrowly missing, or sailed over the edge of the ring because there wasn't enough space.

Angry chimpanzees sat astride their smoking bikes frowning, revving their engines and falling off. The eyes of all the humans watching grew rounder and rounder, and then the chimps started to take it out on each other. The bikes were abandoned and fighting broke out. All the chimps were wearing frilly boy and girl uniforms, and these were the first to go. There was a great flurry of ripping and tearing and soon shredded bits of satin lay all over the studio floor. Then it got even more physical, and lust crept in.

Ed Sullivan was horrified. Here on his show, which went out live to millions and millions of Americans, including that huge and influential area known as the Bible Belt, chimpanzees were doing things to other chimpanzees which should never be shown on television. There was only one solution – bring on the next act. Me!

Chimpanzees were still scattered about the place when, dimly remembering that I had said my grandfather was Welsh, Ed Sullivan announced: 'And now we have a great Welsh singer, from Wales in England – Cilla Black!'

I came on and started to sing *Dancing in the Street.* In the run-throughs I'd done this song as a solo act, but now I soon realized that I wasn't alone. Something was clinging to my leg. It was impossible to ignore it, so I looked down and there was this chimpanzee, who definitely fancied me. I couldn't think what to do except carry on singing until the trainer and studio people finally cleared the floor of randy monkeys. Today I think I would have stopped the band, but there you are. The *Ed Sullivan Show* can have a strange effect on people, as well as chimpanzees.

Also on that same show, by the way, were Debbie Reynolds and Kirk Douglas. I'd like to tell you something about them – only we never met. It was sheer Hollywood the way they handled those people. Almost without anybody seeing how it was done, they were brought into the studio, a magic box was opened and there they were. They did their act and disappeared again. It was almost like pantomime. Speaking of which, I have a few more tales to tell of mayhem in the theatre.

✳✳✳✳

I was in *Aladdin* at the London Palladium when the police came and told us there had been a threat on my life. Apparently someone had phoned in the threat to one of the newspapers. The police took it all very seriously, and Special Branch were drafted in. For a while I could count on Bobby to look after me, but Liverpool were playing in a final at Wembley and he had tickets.

We arrived at the theatre and Bobby was all for more or less pushing me out of the car door and going off to the football. 'Go on, then,' he was saying. 'You'll be all right, love.'

'Sure,' I said, pointing to the huge crowd waiting on the pavement, 'and worrerbout all those people?'

'That's all right, love,' he said. 'Special Branch are in there. They've checked it all out.'

Well, there was no way he was going to miss seeing Liverpool play. So out I got and went to my dressing room, hoping like anything that it was all a hoax. Nothing unusual happened before the curtain went up, and then I concentrated on doing the pantomime. But the rest of the cast had other ideas.

After we had done one or two scenes, I began to notice that no-one else on the stage wanted to come near me. Alfred Marks, for instance, hung about near the wings as much as he could, and if he did have to come close he started to walk about all bent backwards! Basil Brush was in the cast, and even he didn't want to work with me.

Actually, it must have looked very funny. I know that the audience, once they had sussed it out, were roaring with laughter. I just wish it hadn't been me, that's all!

We also had a bomb scare at the Palladium, during an autumn show I was doing there. The police insisted on clearing the theatre and scores of people, including the cast, transferred to the pub across the road where it turned into quite a party. Members of the audience, in ordinary suits and dresses, were chatting away to mysterious orientals in turbans and baggy trousers, holding pints in their hands.

The party ended when someone came into the pub and shouted: 'Anyone for the Palladium?' The artistes trooped across the road and went in through one entrance, and the audience piled in through the main doors. Only now, it was more than a case of full house – it was crammed to overflowing with people who'd decided to leave the local pubs and grab some free entertainment. The management had no way of checking on the audience because people had used their tickets already. 'I don't know,' gatecrashers were saying to confused usherettes. 'I think I was up here somewhere' – and helping themselves to any vacant seat they fancied.

We only heard of one man who didn't go back to see the rest of the show, and that was our accountant who was there with his daughter. 'I never came back,' he told us later when we asked if he'd enjoyed the show. I can't say I blame him; it's not an easy decision, especially if you've got family with you. I know Bobby's first instinct was to look after his kids when we had our other bomb scare.

In Liverpool, I was playing *Dick Whittington* when the police contacted us to say there might be a bomb in the theatre. Bobby was one of the producers of the show and he spoke to the police.

'What do you want us to do?' he asked them.

'Well,' they said, 'strictly you should stop the show.'

'Yes,' said Bobby, 'perhaps we should.' But he wasn't keen. 'Look,' he went on, 'they blew up Lime Street Station the other day. They're not going to come blowing up the theatre.'

He really thought it was unlikely that anyone, however mad, would want to bomb a theatre which seated three thousand people. On the other hand, he wanted to do the right thing by the audience – which included our kids who were in there with Penny, their nanny.

The police had sniffer dogs with them and they searched all the outer parts of the theatre – the foyer, the toilets, and so on, until the only place they hadn't searched was the auditorium.

So then Bobby had an idea. He wanted me to go on and say to the audience that there was a special prize hidden somewhere in the theatre and would everyone please look under their seats. If anyone found something, they shouldn't touch it, just call out and an usherette would come round and give them their present.

Then he said: 'Before you go on and tell them that – let me get our kids out.'

When he had fetched them out, I went on and asked everyone to look under their seat for the special parcel. No-one spoke up, so then I came clean and told them what it was all about. 'We had to ask you to do that,' I said, 'because we had a phone call. Now, if you want to leave, we understand. But if you want to stay, you're very welcome – 'cos *we're* staying.'

There was a big cheer from the audience. Someone called out: 'We're with you, Cilla!' It was getting a bit like World War Two in there. Not one person left, and we put on a lovely pantomime which everyone enjoyed. A few days later, Bobby went to see his Auntie Sarah.

She said: 'I went to see the show, lad.'

'Did you?' said Bobby. 'Why didn't you come round afterwards?'

'Oh, I didn't like to,' she said. 'Anyway, it was at the time of that bomb scare. They had me standing up and looking under the seat – me poor old knees were cracking just like it was a bomb going off. But I couldn't find anything. Still, it was a good show. And do you know what? Only one man left. This little fat feller came down and took his kids out of the audience.'

It was Bobby! And she hadn't recognized him.

'That was me!' he told her.

'It never was!' she gasped.

TIME OFF
IN AUSTRIA

*'The first time I went skiing I wore a short bomber
jacket with knickerbockers and lovely woollen socks –
all straight from the West End. I looked really smart.
First day out, I was learning to walk up the slope
when I fell over. In no time I was soaked through. I
thought: 'I've had enough of this!' I complained to the
instructor. 'I'm freezing cold and wringing wet!'
'Well,' he said. 'Look, at the way you're dressed for a
start.'*

He was quite right. If you bent over in those
little bomber jackets, the back went up and you
were all exposed. In minus temperatures on an
Austrian mountain, that's no joke. What I
should have had was either an all-in-one suit or
a really long jacket.

As for the knickerbockers, they looked as
if they'd be wet through for a week. I looked at
Bobby's trousers. He had a couple of pairs of
proper ski trousers.

I said: 'Tomorrow I'll wear yours.'

The only thing was, I have much longer

legs than Bobby. I didn't really think about it – I just wanted to be warm and dry – until I'd actually pulled on the trousers. Talk about stretch-crutch, it was half-way down to my knees! But at least I was dry and fairly comfortable, and ready to learn to ski.

We were at Lech, in western Austria, invited there in the early Seventies by George Martin and his wife Judy who are real enthusiasts. They've been to a lot of winter resorts but they like Lech because it has so many facilities. At most resorts you have to take the bus if you want to find a good variety of slopes, but at Lech it's all on the spot. Within this one little valley there's a drag chair (a kind of hook you sit on and it tows you up), two cable cars and three chair lifts, all taking you to different ski runs. All of these start within walking distance of the hotel, so there was no need to worry about cars or taxis or any kind of extra transport.

At first we learnt on the baby slopes. I took my time but within a week I could ski well enough to get all the way down without stopping. Bobby went at it a little more boldly and finished up with a sprained ankle because he didn't know how to stop. He does now, but let him tell you about it.

Bobby: 'When you start skiing you keep telling yourself not to fall, you must stay on your feet. So you concentrate on that. But the longer you stay on your skis, the faster you go. Nobody's taught you how to stop, so invariably you're going to fall over sooner or later. The thing to learn is, when you think you're running into trouble – sit down. Then you stop, it's the easiest kind of braking there is. You fall into the snow, then you get up and start again.

Before I knew about this, I was going down the slope at a terrible speed on one leg. I went past this feller who took one look at me and burst out laughing. 'Ah, ha-ha-hah! Ah, ha-ha-haaaah!' I could hear his voice echoing behind me. So that started me off laughing.

I must have looked a right lunatic. Screaming down the slope on one leg, roaring my head off, totally out of control, completely on my own as far as doing anything about it was concerned, and at the same time missing other skiers by inches as I shot past them. The ending was inevitable. I crashed, and at the speed I was doing – a complete novice – I was bound to do myself some damage. I was lucky it was only a sprained ankle.

So then I was off skiing for a couple of days. When I was on my own, I found myself looking through the window up at the top of this mountain, and all I could see was Cilla hurtling downhill in her bomber jacket. "My God!" I was saying to myself. "She's going to fall, she's going to fall," and wincing every time she did a turn. But she didn't fall, she was more sensible.'

George had his moments as well. Although he's a much more experienced skier, he didn't look too comfortable one day as we were going over a series of bumps. It was a fairly flat part of the run, but even there you can pick up a surprising speed. Especially George, who's over six feet tall and wears skis about eight feet long – and there's a lot of friction in sixteen feet of ski. Bobby had already fallen, and then George went backwards, but instead of landing in the snow he found himself squatting on the back of his skis. In no time he was going like a toboggan. Whoosh! He swept past the rest of us, and I'll always remember Judy looking round as her husband swept past with his head about level with her knees.

'George!' she called to him. 'What are you doing down there?'

'I'm trying to get up,' he shouted, and vanished into the distance.

Another time, we were all going up on the chair lift. Bobby used to ride with Judy on the chairs – his story was that they were about equal height and weight, but the main reason was that I would occasionally get excited if the chairs suddenly stopped and left us hanging over a massive drop. Bobby said he couldn't stand the screaming and hysteria, which of course is a terrible exaggeration.

On this particular day I went up with Heinz, the instructor, and George, who's a bit long for chair lifts, went on ahead. Bobby and Judy were at the back. We were nearly at the top, with a huge drop beneath us, when the chairs jerked to a halt and then started going backwards. I looked across and saw that George had missed his turn to jump off and ski down, and so the whole circuit had to be put in reverse. Naturally enough, when I saw it was him I yelled across at him. But Bobby, who thinks he can recognize the sound of me screaming, thought I was going hysterical, and so he was wriggling about in his seat to see if I was still up there somewhere or if I'd finally freaked out and chucked myself into space. But there's not a lot you can do in one of those chairs, so he had to sit and suffer. When the chairs stop, you just sit there completely helpless and half frightened to death with your legs dangling while the chair swings this way and that, the wind whistles past and there's nothing to hang on to except a thin iron bar.

A few minutes later we started off again, and this time we got to the point where you leap off the chair while it's still going, turn, get your balance and ski down – preferably all in one flowing movement. Heinz and I jumped off and skied away. About halfway down we stopped and met up with the others. When Bobby arrived he wanted to know what all the screeching had been about.

George explained that he had been just about to jump off his chair, when he saw that the feller in front of him had dropped a blanket on the snow. George said he was blowed if he was going to risk skiing down and running on to the blanket, he could have broken his neck. So he had stayed on the chair, and the operators had to stop the system and bring him back again, otherwise he would have gone all the way round to the bottom without getting a ski. As we were standing there having a laugh about it, a group of skiers came along. One of them was highly disgusted. He said:

'Did you see that *stupid* Englishman who stayed in his chair! Really!'

It's amazing what you can learn to do in a week. Once we had found our feet a bit, we got into a marvellous daily routine. Unlike summer holidays, where there may be some part of the day which is a bit boring, at a ski resort there's never a dull moment.

Each morning we were up at eight. We had breakfast, got our gear together and we were out on the slopes by ten. We skied till lunchtime, then came back to the hotel and had a super lunch.Our hotel was typically Austrian, so no hamburgers and junk food; all the dishes on the menu were traditional, and beautifully cooked. After lunch, which we'd finish at around two, we went out on the slopes until four-thirty. Back to the hotel, and I'd be tired enough just to want a relaxing shower or a soak in the bath. We'd change, go downstairs for a little Sektorange – in their version that was a blood orange with champagne – and into dinner. After we'd eaten, we either went out to a disco or we'd settle down with George and Judy and get really excited over a game of ludo. By ten o'clock, the day was over, and we were ready for bed.

One night we went by sleigh up to another hotel which had an arrangement with ours so that we could go there for a fondue and their guests could come to our traditional banquet which was held every Friday. We set off in the sleigh and it was magic – better than *Dr Zhivago*. All you heard was the 'jing-jing-jing' of the sleigh bells and the soft thudding of the horses' hooves in the snow. In the moonlight you could see deer coming down from the trees. A wonderful night.

Just above the back of our hotel was a disco. We'd had a very good evening in there with George and Judy – George leaping up and down and headbanging the chandelier. We had a good laugh and one or two Glühweins, then we set out back to the hotel. It was only a few yards, but you had to go down a steep flight of steps which led to the main street. The snow had been falling and we couldn't find where the steps were. Bobby and I both slipped while we were feeling for these invisible steps and slid all the way to the bottom. We weren't hurt, in fact we were shouting and laughing all the way down. As we picked ourselves up, a feller appeared.

'Ey, Cilla,' he said. 'How yer doing? Can I have yer autograph?'

He didn't turn a hair about finding me at the bottom of some steps in a ski resort in Austria. Perhaps he thought I did it all the time!

But we didn't go out every night. At other times, as I mentioned, we stayed in and played ludo. Very fierce some of those games were, too. Not many people have been banned from the ludo board – but I have!

Judy Martin has kept the ludo set that she had when she was a child, so naturally she's very fond of the game. It didn't help matters early on, when Bobby accused her of using loaded dice. She kept throwing double-sixes, and after this had gone on a few times Bobby couldn't resist saying he thought there was something a bit funny about the dice. Judy, who is a super lady, looked horrified, and asked her husband to stick up for her.

'Well, darling,' said George, looking doubtful, 'you *have* been throwing a lot of sixes lately.'

So then Bobby wanted to put her to the test and make her do three trial throws. It might have got a bit serious if we hadn't been laughing so much. You know how these board games can get out of hand.

Then they barred me for interrupting. I couldn't help myself. I was watching everybody else's moves and saying what was going to happen. I didn't help Bobby, which made him mad, but whenever George or Judy threw the dice I'd say something like: 'Ooh, you could land on Bobby.'

They didn't like that. 'Shut up,' they said, very sternly. We played a few rounds in silence, where you could only hear the clicking of the dice, but then I started up again and they banned me from playing!

When we got to Monopoly, it was even worse. Bobby said he could definitely see divorce on the horizon. Later it was all immortalized in song, with lyrics by Ron Goodwin.

He was also in Lech, but shortly before the holiday he'd hurt his ribs and thought he'd better not go skiing. He seemed quite happy about that; in the morning he went off somewhere and had a walk and then met us for lunch. We'd have a laugh together, then we went back to the slopes for more skiing and saw him again in the evening. We didn't always know what he'd been doing during the day, but one evening he said to us:

'Do you know what the German is for brassière?'

'No.'

'Büstenhalter.'

'Oh, is it. Well, that's very interesting, Ron.'

'Yes. Do you know what the German is for knickers?'

'No, what is it?'

'Beinkleider.'

'Get away. How do you know that?'

So now we knew what Ron had been doing with his spare time – looking up naughty words in a German dictionary. That was not all he did. One night we had a birthday party for Bobby, and Ron brought along a new song and sang it to him. It was set to the tune of *Those Magnificent Men In Their Flying Machines* (which he originally wrote), and in the new words he included all the things that happened on our holiday, including the German sausages which Bobby loved and used to keep cold on the ledge outside our window. I was in the song too – for being banned at ludo!

****

When the BBC heard we were going skiing, they weren't very happy about it. 'What happens to the series,' they said, 'if you go and break a leg?'

I had no intention of changing my plans so I told them not to worry, I'd be alright. As if I knew!

But they hadn't finished. 'While you're over there,' they said, 'could you utilize the time (typical BBC) and take some film shots of you skiing, and we'll put them into the show.'

We said yes and Bobby hired a cine camera. One day we took it up to the top of one of the runs, and Bobby said: 'Give me ten minutes to get down to where I can film you, and then follow on.'

It's ever so cold just standing about on a mountain, and I was freezing. As soon as I thought Bobby had had long enough to get ready, I set off.

I skied *beautifully*. I never made any mistakes at all, and once I was down at the bottom I looked around for Bobby. I couldn't see him anywhere at first, but over on one side there was a group of people crowding round something and chattering away in German, so I went to have a look. They were pulling this figure out of a wall of snow. It had got embedded in there, with its arms stuck out sideways – a bit like the figure in a Crucifixion scene. Then I saw the beard, and I knew who it was.

Bobby: 'What happened was, I thought I'd ski down quick to be ready to film Cilla. I went off, with the camera round my neck. The run had a lot of little bumps in it, and each time I came to one of these I did a turn and zig-zagged away at an angle.

Then a little French feller came up alongside, and started skiing exactly level with me. Each time I turned, he turned. I thought: "I'm going to get away from him, he's dangerous." But I couldn't. We were going down the slope like Siamese twins. It was uncanny; if we'd tried to do it on film it would

54

have taken years of practice to get it so perfect.

I started to lose my temper. "Will you get lost!" I was shouting at him, and he was looking offended and gabbling something I couldn't understand. All this looking sideways and shouting must have upset my sense of direction. I did another turn and went straight into a wall of snow.

I must have gone in about four feet. To get me out, people were pulling on my ankles and that was having the effect of tipping my head further in. When I was finally out I looked a terrible mess. The mad *Engländer*-Willis of the Antarctic – with the camera still hanging from my neck.

Another thing, by the way, that you don't want to do when you're out on the slopes is to be taken short. One afternoon I was up on the mountain and desperate to spend a penny. I didn't know what to do. Judy was the nearest to me out of our party, and as she was more experienced in how to behave in the mountains, I asked her.

"That's all right, Bobby," she said. "Go over there, by that mound of snow."

"Fine," I said, thinking to myself that if Judy said it was alright, it must be. Even if it wasn't alright, I was going to do something pretty quick. So I went over to this mound and got to work. First of all, in these situations, you've got your ski trousers to deal with, then there's your thermal underwear, then your ordinary underwear. When you're out skiing, it takes forever to get ready for a tinkle.

Anyway, there I was at last . . . and, oh, the sheer relief of it. Marvellous. Then, half-way through the performance, I looked up just as a party of schoolchildren came skiing past. There I was, in full view. I couldn't stop and I couldn't hide what I was doing.

The teacher nodded in sympathy as he went past and said something like "Ho ho." So at least he wasn't offended. Even if he was, I didn't have much choice. When you've gotta go, you've gotta go!'

✳✳✳✳

Lech is a wonderful place, but not easy to get to. You fly to Zürich, then you take a train which weaves in and out of the mountains for hours, or you can hire a van and drive yourself there.

Our first time out there, we went by train, but we were soon cured of that after we'd shared a compartment with a man who, if he wasn't picking his nose, was breaking wind. He kept it up for hours, and the expression on his face didn't change once – it was totally blank. Well, imagine that in a crowded train compartment which was kept at a stifling temperature so you wouldn't believe there was snow outside. One journey like that was enough for us, and ever since we've gone by road.

On the return journey the road takes you back to the airport, and then of course you're hoping there'll be a plane to fly you to London. Sometimes there is, but not always. One year, the runway was frozen and all the airlines decided to stay on the ground. Except one – Air India.

Bobby, George and Judy all looked at me, the flying expert. They were quite happy to get on this Frozen Curry Special, but before they did they wanted my agreement.

I said: 'You must be joking. What do Indians know about ice conditions?' (For the moment I forgot that India also has a few bumps in its landscape, e.g. the Himalayas.) 'You can go if you want to,' I told them, 'but I'm staying till the weather is better.'

We stayed the night in Zürich. Next day there was no improvement, so we decided to catch a train to Paris and get a flight from there. By then we had no more time to spare because I had to be back in London for work.

At the station, I got on the train with Judy and Bobby and all our luggage, but when we looked round there was no sign of George. Bobby said he would go and find him, so he got out and walked up the platform towards the station buildings = and as he did so, the train started moving off. As soon as he saw what was happening, he ran after us. I was leaning out of the window and calling to him, but he was falling further and further behind. Then he stopped, and the train pulled away from the station with me and Judy on board, Bobby on the platform with my passport and all our money, and George nowhere.

Left on his own, Bobby thought he'd probably check into a hotel and do some phoning to find out what was going on. He was still thinking about this when he bumped into. . .

'George!!!'

For the second time in only a few minutes, George did his thin air trick, and reappeared in front of Bobby just as suddenly as he'd disappeared on the way to the train. Together they went along to the stationmaster's office and got them to telephone down the line to get a message to me and Judy. Then they settled down to a four-hour wait for the next train.

Meanwhile, Judy, who's very Roedean and doesn't flap easily, was marvellous. She didn't waste any time at all. While I was sitting there thinking: 'Oh, God, what's going to happen?' Judy had spotted someone.

'Don't I know you?' she called to this feller.

'Oh, hello Judy,' he said, 'and where are you off to?'

'We're going to Paris,' she said. She had already assumed that everything would be alright, even if she had temporarily lost her husband, so when she found that this feller was also stopping off in Paris, she was arranging for us all to have lunch with him the next day.

At Basle, Judy and I got off the train, and I went with the luggage and sat in the left-luggage office. Judy said: 'Won't be a minute,' and disappeared. The next thing she did was to find out that the local airport was open, and then she booked all four of us on a flight to London. How anyone can be so organized in a crisis beats me, but Judy took the whole thing completely in her stride. She was quite right, of course. Everything did come out OK. Bobby and George arrived on the next train and were shown into the Lost-and- Found section of the left-luggage office – and were reunited with their wives. The contrasting reactions of the two wives was fairly interesting, too.

'Oh, hello, Poopie,' said Judy to George in a bright but matter-of-fact way. Meanwhile, I felt like bursting into tears. Oh, to have had a Roedean education!

****

These skiing memories date back to a time before and just after we started a family. In those days there weren't the facilities for taking young children on a winter sports holiday. Even now, although Lech has got a super new swimming pool where you can bathe and watch the skiers through the windows, I think that resorts like Lech are really built around skiing, and there isn't enough to do for someone who doesn't want to spend all their mornings and afternoons out on the slopes.

So for some years we have given skiing a miss. But now that the boys are bigger – and Robert, who's fifteen, can ski already – I'm dying to get back there and have another go. Next Easter, I hope – but not in a bomber jacket and knickerbockers!

Family snaps from Lech, in Austria. That's Penny, our nanny, with me and Robert.

Proof- if proof were needed – that I am Cilla Black and that black thing behind me is The Bitch!

Safely home in London after our Australian tour of 1975, with Robert (4) and Ben (11 months). This was the trip where our Jumbo jet lost an engine on the outward journey.

Two very good Australian friends, TV personalities Mike Walsh (left) and John Michael Howson. In his lapel John is wearing an Australian flag which Ben made for him when he came over to the UK for the wedding of Prince Charles and Lady Di.

We had a big barbecue at the house for the Aussies, Bobby flew the Australian flag for the day and Ben drew this little souvenir for John, who was so delighted that he wore it on Australian television and told the viewers: 'Look what Ben Willis made for me.'

AUSTRALIA

'On my 1985 tour you'd think the Sixties had never gone away. I went on a TV chat show and they asked me what had happened to all my contemporaries. What a daft question. Half of them were on the same show!'

Australia is no longer the remote place it used to be at the end of the Fifties, when it took three days to fly from London to Sydney and a lot of people went there by boat. On that afternoon chat show they had The Shadows, The Bachelors, Freddie Garrity and myself. A lot of the groups do very well over there with a seven or eight-week season, and for some reason there was a whole bunch of us there at the same time.

It's not just groups, and not just groups who first came through in the Sixties. In the same hotel as me were Spandau Ballet, Max

Bygraves and Michael Parkinson – in fact it was just like being in an English hotel. That's what's funny about Australia – in many ways it's very very different from home, and yet you hardly ever feel you're in a *foreign* country.

When you fly out there, you leave London and you land first stop in Bahrain. There's not much doubt that Bahrain is foreign, with all those Arabs floating about. From there you go to Singapore, you feel the hot atmosphere and the locals there are Chinese so you know you're in a foreign country. You get back on the plane and you land in Sydney – and it's like you've gone right round the globe and come home again instead of going half-way across it. Everyone understands everyone, and people call out 'Hi, Cilla' as if I'd just come from round the corner.

And whatever the Australians may say about being fiercely independent of us, you see far more of the Royal Family on their television than you do at home. When we were last over there, we watched the Queen's tour of Portugal. The Australians were obsessed by it.

At the same time, they are a very proud people. A small example of this is the number of signs you see in restaurants saying 'No Tipping Please'. I agree with that. People like hotel staff shouldn't have to grovel to the customers in order to make up their wage to a decent level. They should be paid a decent wage in the first place.

Something that never seems to change is the Australians' 'superior' attitude towards us, and by us I mean the 'Whingeing Poms'. In fact the British in exile are now known as 'Piles' (They came out, they won't go back, and they're a pain in the bum). All I can say is that the British I meet in Australia couldn't care less. When you do a concert you don't know how many Brits are in the audience, but it's safe to assume that ninety per cent or more are established Australians. This didn't stop one feller in the front row from shouting up to me that he was from Liverpool.

'How long have you been here?' I asked him.

'Too bloody long,' he said, loud and clear, and got a big laugh.

Good for him, I thought, but if a foreigner said that in England it wouldn't be taken so lightly. People would be waiting for him outside, and if they didn't actually hit him their attitude would be angry. 'Go on,' they'd tell him, 'we'll give you your old banana boat back. Just get on it and clear off.'

It's certainly true that the Liverpool Australians will never admit they come from anywhere but Liverpool, even if they've been over there for more than twenty years. The best case was an old feller in his nineties. We were in the Sydney Opera House, more than ten years ago, and when I asked him how long he'd been in Australia he said it was over eighty years.

'Do you think you'll settle?' I asked him.

He'd gone over in a sailing ship in the wool trade, carrying coal for ballast till they got there. He wanted me to sing a Liverpool shanty, so I sang him *Liverpool Lullaby* and he was well pleased.

✳✳✳✳

I've been going to Australia since 1965, and it's obviously come on a lot in terms of the buildings and the general prosperity. When I first arrived, the airport building was a corrugated shed with a fan in the ceiling; now it's as up to date as anywhere. But whatever the Australians do to make their lives more comfortable, they'll never change the incredible wildlife they have there – and I don't mean just in the Outback.

In Tamworth the Mayor and the Chief of Police and the local big-wigs put on a dinner for the crew on our show. It was all very nice, they'd made a special effort, and we sat down to this Chinese meal. (Bobby says he still can't work out which part of China the chef came from, but that's beside the point.) We were sitting there, and one of the girls brought me a salad. She'd just put the plate in front of me, when Bomp! A huge flying cockroach landed smack in the salad. There was green stuff everywhere!

Then you start to notice them all over the place. My eyesight is not the best in the world, but once you're tuned in to flying cockroaches you see them all the time. Apparently they were having a special plague of them at the time. The locals didn't seem to mind, they took them in their stride. They already had a special gesture – the Aussie wave – which they use to carry on a conversation with only the shortest of pauses while they brush away the latest insect. Usually this is a fly, but it works just as well with flying cockroaches. For example: 'That's right, Cilla (wave), we have those (wave) over here (wave) as well.'

Just before we went out on our last trip they had a plague of mice that I wasn't sorry to miss. Billions of mice running everywhere, and nothing the Aussies could do about them. They swept through the farms, eating everything, jumping about in swarms. The only thing that killed them off was the climate: once the temperature had dropped far enough, their fantastic breeding rate slowed down and the humans got back in control.

Usually on a tour the venues are in the big cities, and the best way to get from one to the next is by plane. That way you don't see much of the country, and so one year we did a proper country tour. We played Wagga Wagga, and Ballarat, the centre of the 1851 gold rush, and we visited the place where Ned Kelly had a famous shoot-out and saw his armour. It meant being on the road for three or four hours a day on top of the time we had to put in rehearsing and doing the show, but it was a great experience.

Australia is the only place I know where you find big emus dashing along beside the road, and going as fast as you are. And little koalas sitting about the place. Scores of kangaroos, of course, and parrots flying everywhere. I found it incredible that there were so many parrots in the wild. Sometimes you could look across the fields and see a great white mass heaving about, which turned out to be a flock of cockatoos eating some poor farmer's entire crop in about twenty minutes. They chew wood as well, and recently I read that a bunch of cockatoos were invading the suburbs of Sydney and eating people's window-sills. Someone must have told them they were a protected species and they've got cheeky about it, because by law you aren't allowed to capture a cockatoo in the wild and take it home. If you want a cockatoo as a pet you have to buy one that's been bred in captivity.

Talking of wildlife, I also ran into Robert Morley while I was in Australia. We were staying in Sydney at the Sebel Town House, which is very good about looking after show-business people and the funny hours we keep.

They have a pool on the roof and one day I went up there. Although I may make a bit of noise on-stage, away from the theatre I like to be quiet. I'm certainly not the type to parade around a pool saying 'Look at me' to everybody. I like to put on my sunhat and dark glasses and just be alone.

So there I was. I found myself a nice chair and settled down. Suddenly I heard this voice blaring: 'Cilla! Daaarling!'

Everybody turned round. I looked up – and there he was. The human water buffalo.

'Robert,' I said. 'How are you?'

'What, dear? What?'

'H-h-how are you,' I repeated, trying to keep my voice down, not wanting to start a public performance. Fat chance.

'I'm sorry, dear,' bellowed Robert, 'I'm getting on a bit now. Can you speak more clearly' (his way of asking me to speak proper, no doubt). 'Cilla, darling,' he went on, 'you look *marvellous!'*

There was nothing for it, if he couldn't understand me, I'd have to speak up. All around us on the roof people were raising their heads from their books, adjusting their sunglasses and getting into a comfortable listening position.

'Your television show, darling, is absolutely wonderful,' Robert went on. 'What's it called?'

'*Surprise Surprise,'* I said.

'Whaat?' he roared.

'*Surprise Surprise,'* I repeated.

'It's wonderful, darling,' he shouted. 'You MUST LET ME COME ON IT!'

Then he had a bit of a moan about one of his advertising contracts. I won't go into the details because I don't want the company suing me, but if you do want to know more you can ask anybody who was on the roof of the hotel that day. They must have had the whole story drilled into their memories, complete with cries of 'What swine! They never offered *me* that!' and other colourful show-business expressions.

Then, suddenly, like a glass of champagne in a heatwave, he was gone. Evaporated. Well, not completely evaporated, I hope. But anyway, he went his way and I went mine, and we didn't meet again on that tour. But it's one of the perks of our business that you can have these chance encounters, like on a rooftop in Sydney, which last for five minutes but keep you smiling for days afterwards.

As for our country travelling arrangements, I must tell you about the bus we toured with – The Bitch. That's what they call it, don't ask me why. If you want to hire it, you ring up the bus company and say: 'Can I have The Bitch?' If you're lucky, and it's free, you get this amazing all-black luxury coach with dark windows, big settees, a bar, video . . . The only thing was, they fixed our touring sign across the back of the bus, so if you were driving along behind us this is what you would read:

YOU ARE FOLLOWING
"THE BITCH"
ON TOUR WITH
CILLA BLACK

✱✱✱✱

I missed out on New Zealand this time, which I was sorry about. They have some venues over there which you have to say are spectacular even if they don't always work too well. In one city we played out of doors in what looked like a copy of the Hollywood Bowl. The stage was shaped like a shell, and in front of it was a pond, with the audience all banked up on the other side. Not very good for us, because in my act I need contact with the audience so I can chat with them.

To make it a little better, we moved all our stage gear to the back of the stage and had a few rows of seats put in at the front. So far so good – except that it rained all day long. I thought it was going to be a washout, but far from it. Eleven thousand people turned up for the show. I, meanwhile, changed in a caravan and went on-stage in a trouser suit.

We were terrified of electrical problems, what with the rain and being outdoors, so we pulled the mikes back as far as we could and got on with it. Luckily it all went off with no problems.

Still in the Great Outdoors, we once played a swimming pool in Perth. It was a big, Olympic-sized pool and they didn't board it over; instead they erected a bandstand between the end of this big pool and two smaller pools. The audience sat in the pool spectator seats along one side, and again it was the same problem of no contact, so we had some seats put down just by the bandstand.

It never occurred to us to ask them to shut the pool while we rehearsed; we just thought they would do it automatically. Unfortunately, it had never occurred to them to do any such thing, so when we came to rehearse there were kids swimming past under my nose, doing saucy bits of synchro to our string orchestra. We had a wind that day as well, so the music kept lifting off the stands and blowing into the water!

Sydney Opera House is a marvellous building. Even so, if you were standing outside your dressing room and you heard your opening music, there is no way you'd be able to find the stage in time. Unless you had a guide, I doubt if you'd even make it for your second song. It's all wonderful and elegant, with thick thick carpets and very plush-looking, but you'd be nowhere without the security guard who leads you along passageways, round corners, into a lift, out again, more passageways. . . At least you're warmed up when you get there.

For me, the most luxurious venue in Australia is the Melbourne Concert Hall. It's a later building than the Sydney Opera House, and in fact I was the first show in there, the day after the official opening which was a very big do with fireworks. It's very impressive, with a magnificent room that seats two thousand. And the dressing room suite is like a set from *Dynasty*. You almost wonder if the designers hadn't just come from watching a few de-luxe American soap operas when they drew up the plans for it.

In most of the Australian cities the facilities are much better than they used to be. In Perth they've built a superb new concert hall, and there's also a fine one in Adelaide – where, in the old days, we used to appear in a basketball stadium. So for the touring performer it's a much more impressive picture than it used to be.

I was at a new club complex in Newcastle, which is situated not far from Sydney and is a bit like our Newcastle in that it's a very industrial area. This new club gives its members a terrific deal – big concert hall, swimming pool, billiard room with about twenty tables, squash courts, cinemas, three restaurants, plus a gambling saloon which subsidizes the seat prices when they have people like me going in there.

It's a great club, with marvellous facilities – except for one thing. There were three super dressing rooms, but they only had one entrance and that was through the star dressing room. So everyone else – the band, the comic who'd been on before – all had to file through my dressing room. Still . . . that's show business.

But I do like going there, and I do feel comfortable with the Aussies. If it wasn't for the fact that I have to leave my boys behind for the six or eight weeks of a tour, I would be glad to stay longer and explore the country a bit more. The other nice thing is that the Australians always give me a lovely welcome. As a lady said to me in Darwin at the start of a tour:

'I know they call you "Our Cilla" over there, but you're "Our Cilla" here as well.'

THE JOY OF
FLYING

'I look at people on planes and I think: "They're not long for this world, I'm sure something's going to happen!" Mind you, they're probably looking at me and thinking exactly the same thing.'

I am not really a superstitious person, but I do believe in omens. If I went to the airport and the flight was cancelled, I wouldn't take the next one. I would think that someone was trying to tell us something, and we would be silly not to listen.

Ever since the first time I got in a plane, for a short trip to Paris, I have never found flying easy. It was a classic how-we-used-to-fly journey and I have never forgotten it. I got on the plane and the air hostess came round with the sweeties – remember them? We took off and

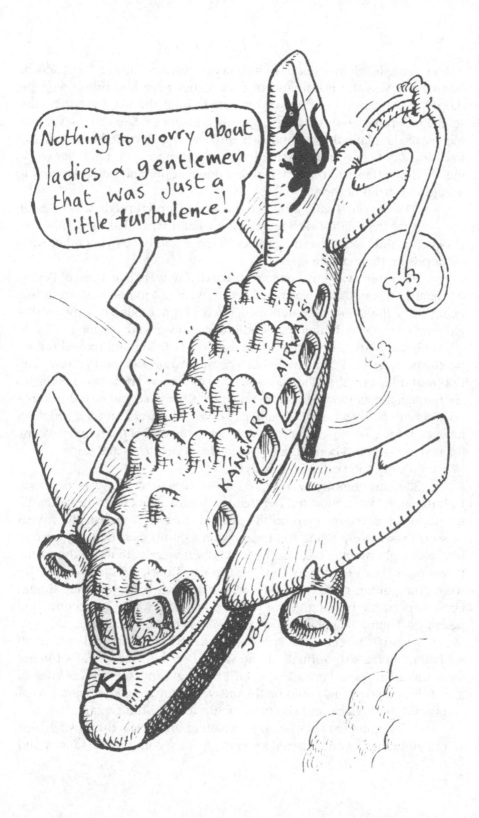

almost immediately ran into bad turbulence. I wasn't afraid, I just accepted that this was the norm, and that all flights were like riding on a big dipper at the fairground. As we bucketed about the sky the air hostess staggered up the aisle carrying a tray of sandwiches. She came level with me just as the plane threw another fit and she was flung to her knees. Not knowing any better, and thinking the poor girl must spend half her working life doing these acrobatics, I smiled down at her and helped myself to a sandwich from her tray.

'Thank you,' I said, a bit like the Queen, and turned away to eat it.

After that flight I decided I knew what it was all about. Only with experience did I learn that the airlines of the world have many other ways of surprising their customers.

In a funny way, my first reactions to flying were like those of Penny, our nanny. When Robert was three, we all went out to South Africa. It was Penny's first flight and, although she looked a bit nervous, she's the kind of girl who takes everything in her stride so she never said anything.

It was dark when we left the terminal building and moved out towards the runway. Penny was with Robert on one side of the aisle, and Bobby and I sat on the other side – four seats across. There was nothing to see through the windows, but from under the floor we could hear the bomp-bomp-bomp of the wheels crossing the tarmac. This went on for a couple of minutes at least, because it's a long way out to the end of the runway. Penny listened to it – bomp-bomp-bomp – then she turned to us and said:

'It's not too bad, is it, this flying?'

She had completely accepted that this was what it was all about. Unfortunately, we had to tell her that the best was yet to come. After all, it's smoother in the air than on the ground. Isn't it? Well, usually. A year or so later, we were flying to Singapore in a Jumbo jet. Ben, my second boy, was eight months old, and he and Robert were with us on the plane. It was night, but I couldn't sleep. Next to me, Bobby was fast asleep. We were going along quite smoothly when suddenly I heard a dull thump like a supersonic boom and the whole plane shook and seemed to skid sideways. Then it straightened up and went on flying as before.

I wasn't especially worried about it because it looked as though we had gone back to normal. All the same, I couldn't sleep. Earlier in the flight the air hostess had asked if I'd like to go and see the cockpit, so now I decided that this could be the answer to my sleepless night. I went and found the hostess and she took me up to meet the captain.

A few minutes later we were chatting and I asked him what that 'boom' noise had been. 'I thought you might have come on the tannoy and told us about it,' I said. I often say this to airline people because I feel there is a lot they could tell the public and put their minds at rest rather than saying nothing and leaving them to stew. When there is turbulence, for instance, it's much better to explain this to the passengers and not just leave it, then ten minutes later switch on the 'FASTEN SEAT BELTS' sign which gets some people in a high old panic.

'Well,' said the captain, looking a bit doubtful, 'I couldn't very well come on the tannoy and say we'd lost an engine, could I?'

Pilots must think that show-business people are alien creatures who don't have the same kind of feelings as ordinary people. A bit like pilots, really. If he'd searched the whole plane, he couldn't have found a worse person to confide in. I managed to carry on with the conversation, and not let the panic show, even though on the inside I was all in knots. It was getting like some kind of mad tea party, where people battle away talking a lot of polite rubbish with a smile on their face while underneath the surface great dramas are unfolding.

Instead of shouting 'Oh, my God!' I heard myself say: 'But that's all right, because these things can land on two engines, can't they?'

It must have been something I'd heard from Bobby.

'Oh yes,' said the captain. Then he added: 'Provided we don't lose the other engine on that side of the plane, because they have to balance each other.'

He was doing it again! Confiding in me. *Me!* If he'd just said 'Yes', I'd have been happy with that. But he had to go on and tell me that if the other engine on that side blew, we'd be in real trouble.

'My God,' I thought to myself, 'this is dreadful.' Something else was bothering me – I have a fear of crashing in water. I don't mind the idea of going into the side of a mountain, but I'd hate to go down in the sea. So I asked how long we'd been flying.

'Three hours,' he said.

'And how much longer is there to go?'

'Four and a half hours.'

'Ah, yes,' I said, 'but it's all over land, isn't it?'

'No,' he said, 'it's all over the sea.'

I thought it was time I got out of the cockpit before he told me something else I didn't want to know. So I thanked him very much, went down to my seat and woke Bobby.

'Bobby! Bobby!' I said to him in an awed whisper, *'we've lost an engine.'*

He didn't seem to mind at all. 'Go and tell Vic about it,' he said, and turned his head away and closed his eyes.

I went back to the smoking section where Vic, our agent, was sitting. I woke him up. 'Oh, Vic,' I said, 'I've got something really terrible to tell you.'

'Oh,' he said, 'what's wrong? What's wrong? Is it one of the children?' He thought maybe one of our boys had been taken ill.

'No,' I said, 'we've lost an engine.'

Vic, who was known to be a nervous flyer, went white. Within seconds he had great beads of sweat standing out on his face. Then he was mopping himself with a handkerchief and trying to excuse it by saying he must have eaten something which had upset his stomach.

So he was no use. I went back to my seat and waited for the hours to tick by. At last it was morning, no other 'booms' shook the peacefulness of the cabin, and shortly we would be preparing to land. Now the captain had to break his silence because at the airport they would be treating us as an emergency and lining the runway with fire trucks. He came on the air. 'Now get out of this,' I thought to myself.

'Good morning, ladies and gentlemen,' he began. 'I hope you all had a good night's sleep. Shortly we shall be landing in Singapore. During the night you may have been aware of a noise coming from the left wing of the aircraft. That was the moment when one of our engines failed. There is no need for you to worry about this because the aircraft is functioning perfectly normally. On the ground, when we land, you will see that the emergency services have been brought out. This is simply a precautionary measure, and no cause for alarm.'

'Well that's all right,' I remember thinking. 'At least we've reached Singapore.'

The only thing was, with this captain there always had to be a punchline in any remark he made. 'However,' he went on, 'we do recommend that you take out your false teeth, take off your high-heeled shoes and remove any pointed objects you may be carrying or wearing . . .'

'He's at it again,' I said to Bobby, as we stripped for landing. 'There's no panic, but he does recommend we do all this!'

When we did finally land, I was incredibly relieved. Sitting in a Jumbo jet for four and a half hours, waiting for a second engine to fail, is not a relaxing way to travel.

✳✳✳✳

We were flying British Airways to Australia. We went from London to Zürich, waited there for an hour or so to pick up more passengers, and then we were set to go. The plane taxied out to its starting position, and after a short pause the brakes were off and we moved down the runway, gathering speed. Soon we were racing along really fast, close to the speed you go at just before takeoff – when the pilot suddenly slammed on the brakes.

The aborted take-off must be one of the most terrifying things you can experience in a passenger aircraft. One moment you are hurtling along the runway, waiting for that familiar lurch as you lift off and the wheels stop banging on the tarmac, then the next moment the top half of your body is trying to separate itself from the bit wearing the seat belt, while your hands grab for the arm rests and cling on like crazy, your eyes bulge and your teeth clench like Dracula's dentist. You might feel a fool looking like that, but you don't care. And you don't look too much of a fool anyway because, all around you, three hundred and fifty other punters are doing exactly the same thing, wondering if *their* last moment has come.

It was like World War Three in there as we screeched and squealed along the runway. The noise was incredible. The doors of the luggage compartments above our heads sprang open and coats and bags and bottles were flying everywhere. Meanwhile, in your mind you're waiting. It took an agonizing time to bring the plane under control, and during that time we never knew if we were going to crash into something or whether we'd be okay.

When it was all over, we taxied back to the terminal building where we had to wait twelve hours while the airline found a new plane for us. Apparently, it was only a small electrical fault which had triggered the emergency light in the cockpit and forced the pilot to abort the take-off. The airline assured us that we would have been alright if the pilot had carried on and taken off. All the same, their engineers couldn't repair the fault and so the whole plane had to be taken out of service. It makes you wonder what's going on, doesn't it?

Sometimes I wonder why I ever get on a plane at all. Bobby says it's the safest way to travel, but there are days when it nearly freaks me out and I feel I only do it as a way of persuading myself that I'm not that frightened, and I must get over my fears.

Today, if I get the jitters, I try and think of my favourite plane – and I've no trouble remembering which one that is. Concorde. The best possible way to fly. I've been on it a few times now, and on one journey we went to Singapore with a stop-off to refuel at Bahrain. Each leg of the journey took about four hours, and it was fantastic. No jet-lag when you get there, and no turbulence on the way – because you're so high up and shooting through the deep-blue sky so fast, there's no time for any of that. You can literally stand a

50p coin on edge on the table in front of you, it's that smooth. And the Dom Perignon helps as well!

The only trouble we had was in explaining to Robert – as the speed of the plane came up on the computer display – how he could possibly be going through the air faster than a bullet from a rifle without feeling sick! In fact, he wasn't too sure about getting back on board in Bahrain for another dose of Mach 2, but then he may have had other reasons.

He may have been thinking about the time his journey to the Moon was aborted. At Disneyworld, near Los Angeles, he'd got on this rocket which they said was going to the Moon. Everyone sat in a seat like an airline seat, but when the rocket 'took off you not only got the full sound effects, the seat kind of sucked you in as if you really were tearing into space. Then, as you approached the Moon, the whole thing started shaking like mad. Then a message came over the tannoy: 'Mission aborted. Return to Earth immediately.'

So, with that as his background to supersonic travel, it's hardly surprising that Robert felt a bit freaked out on Concorde. Would we abort? Were we really going that fast? Won't something go wrong? That rocket never got there, did it?

✳✳✳✳

On our last trip to Australia we flew just about every day. A lot of the flights were short, one-hour hops and that was part of the problem. The planes couldn't go up very high and it was almost impossible to avoid turbulance at these lower altitudes, because that is the level at which the hot air meets the cold and sets up a belt of disturbed atmosphere. One really bouncy journey was up to Cairns in northern Queensland; for reasons that will become apparent, Bobby will have to tell the story.

Bobby: 'We were only in the air a few minutes before we started to bump and bounce around. I looked across at Cilla, expecting to see the white knuckles gripping the arm rests and wondering what I could say to try and calm her down – but she was asleep! It was the most amazing thing, because she was jolting around with the rest of us, and I know I was lifted off the seat several times; but she stayed fast asleep until we got there.

The climate around that part of Queensland is tropical and they seem to get extreme turbulence with every flight. The reason Cilla slept was that we had got up at six that morning to catch an early flight, missed it and booked ourselves on another one at noon. By the time we got on the plane,

Cilla was tired from all the to-ing and fro-ing and dropped off to sleep. It's just as well she did, otherwise she wouldn't have wanted to do the show that night.'

On another flight in Australia we actually went into a nosedive! I'm sure we must have had a student driver that day. When we took off, we were only on the runway for two seconds and then – zooom! We were in the air, the plane was pointing straight upwards like a rocket and all the passengers were leaning backwards with their knees in the air.

We were flying to Canberra from Sydney, and there were a lot of politicians on board. I don't know whether our friend the pilot was trying to impress them, but he was certainly having an effect on me. As soon as we flattened out at our flying height I found myself calling for champagne! Officially it was the breakfast flight, and I had some breakfast as well, but it was the glass of bubbly that I needed most.

When we came in to land it was the same story in reverse. Canberra is set in a ring of surrounding hills, and that may be why our pilot wanted nothing to do with a gentle, angled descent. We attacked Canberra like a Japanese dive-bomber. Suddenly the plane flipped through about ninety degrees and started roaring into the earth. As Canberra jumped up to meet us, I said to Bobby:

'It's going too fast!'

Bobby, whose job it is to keep me calm at such moments, was speechless. I thought to myself: 'This has gotta be it.' But it wasn't. Somehow the pilot did another back-breaking turn, and we hurtled into the capital of Australia.

It wasn't only me who thought it had been a hair-raising flight. As I got off the plane, a feller turned to me and said:

'Blimey, that was a bit fierce.'

And *he* looked like a regular customer!

✳✳✳✳

Another small reservation I have about flying is that some airline staff are not exactly flexible when it comes to rules and regulations. Maybe it's the uniform that makes them fancy themselves so much, and put on superior attitudes, but frankly there have been one or two I could have strangled.

I was promoting a new album and the record people wanted me to go up to Glasgow for a radio show. Bobby and I got to Heathrow and found there was a delay on the shuttle service. Some time went by, which was irritating for us because the show was going out live, and by the time we boarded the plane our schedule was looking a little too tight for comfort, although we would have made it to the broadcasting studio in time if the plane had taken off there and then.

It didn't. We sat there, on the end of the terminal arm, for twenty minutes, thirty minutes, forty. . .

I said to Bobby: 'By the time we get there, I'll have missed the radio show. So then we'll just have to turn round and come back again. It's a waste of time going up there. Bobby, I want to get off this plane.'

By now all the doors were locked. Bobby, who's so lovely and nice and doesn't like making a fuss, said: 'You can't, love. Not now.'

But I was getting more and more determined, as every second went by, that this was a ridiculous situation and we had to get off the plane. I told the stewardess, then the steward, then some other feller with stripes on his jacket. They didn't want to know. I explained the whole situation. We were still attached to the terminal arm, so there was no need to go fetching ladders or anything that would delay the other passengers any more than they'd already been delayed. Why couldn't we simply walk off?

Nothing. It wasn't allowed. As far as these people were concerned, we might have been halfway to the moon, they were not going to open the door. No matter what I said, they weren't going to budge. Meanwhile, I was getting crosser and crosser about the whole business. I looked at Bobby in disbelief, and he came to my rescue.

If we have an arrangement about how we persuade people to see our point of view, I'm the one who fires the bullets, while Bobby is reasonable. Now he started in on them:

'There's no point in us staying on the plane. Open the door, please, and let us get off.'

Not a flicker from the flight people, who were giving us a dose of the Russian guards. So Bobby went on:

'Look. There's no point in us going to Scotland to appear in a live radio programme which we've now missed because we've been sitting on this tarmac for forty minutes. There's no point in going up there. It means wasting several hours of our time, and it's also a waste of money because we don't need to make the journey. Can you let us off, please.'

'You can still come back the same night,' the feller insisted.

'Yes,' said Bobby, 'but there's no point in us going up there in the first place if all we're going to do is turn round and come back again.'

Finally, finally, they came round to our point of view and we got off the plane. But the fuss they made – fetching the Airport Police to give us an

escort – was incredible. I know they have to have good security at air-
ports, but they shouldn't treat the travelling public like prisoners. As for
the shuttle being a 'walk-on, walk-off service – tell that to the birds.

Bobby and I had another run-in with the airport authorities when we
came back from a holiday in France. We don't enjoy doing this, by the way,
and we always reckon we have to take a lot more than we dish out. But
there are times, when we *know* we are in the right, that we think it's stupid
just to lie down and let these officials walk all over us; so we put in a protest.

We had Robert with us, when he was small, and we were taking
him around in one of those folding buggies, which were fairly new at the
time. Going out, the airline wouldn't let us take the buggy on the plane as
hand luggage, so it had to go in the hold with the main baggage.

To make life as easy as we could – what with all our other bags
and baby things, not to mention Robert himself, we asked if they would
put the buggy in the hold last and bring it out first, so that when we came
down the steps in France they could just hand it to us and we could push
Robert to the terminal building instead of having to carry him.

'That's no problem,' they said. And they were as good as their
word. We collected the buggy at the foot of the steps as we got off the
plane. Fine. We had our holiday, and on the way back we asked if they'd
do the same thing. 'That's no problem,' they said – and the buggy was
loaded last so it could be first out at Heathrow.

We landed at Heathrow, and Bobby said to the head steward: 'I'd
like to pick up our baby buggy which was loaded last in France.'

'Oh, no,' said the steward. 'You can't do that. It has to be unloaded
with the rest of the luggage.'

I know it comes off with the rest of the luggage,' said Bobby, 'but
the point is, the feller's put it on last in France so we . . .'

'That's not possible,' said the steward sharply. 'It has to be unloaded by authorized baggage handlers along with the rest of the luggage.
You'll have to go through to the Baggage Hall and wait for it there.'

Bobby turned to me. 'Right, Cilla,' he said. 'You just sit there.'

I sat down again and Bobby joined me. Along came the steward.
'What are you doing?' he asked.

'I'm staying on the plane here until you take my pram off and give
it to me.'

'You can't do that.'

'I *am* doing it.'

'But look,' he said. 'We've flown you all the way over here . . .'

'I know,' said Bobby. 'I paid for you to do that. Now will you just do me a favour and get my pram for me.'

Pause for thought. The feller didn't really know what to do, so he sent for the Airport Police.

'What's the problem here?' asked the Red Hat, strolling into the cabin.

'We flew out to France,' said Bobby, 'and we were able to get the buggy for the baby. Now we've come back, and we want it again.'

'Is that all?' said Red Hat.

'Yes,' said Bobby, 'we want our buggy. Can we have it, please.'

'Certainly you can,' said Red Hat. A minute or so later, we were pushing Robert off the plane in his buggy. The steward was furious.

I hope, by the way, that when this book comes out I'm not going to be given the cold shoulder by all those airline staff who have looked after me and Bobby so well for something like twenty years. It's a funny thing about flying that you remember the alarming bits for ever, but you immediately forget all the successful flights where you felt relaxed and the whole thing passed off smoothly.

I am not saying that flying no longer makes me nervous, because to some extent I think it always will. But having children with me has helped to give me a calmer outlook. I find it's much better if I have some-one to look after rather than sitting there with nothing to do except worry – and pester Bobby with questions.

Questions like: 'Why hasn't that sign come on?' or 'Why doesn't that sign go out?' or 'Why has it gone out?'

It's amazing what a little bit of fear can do. Still, if the stories in this chapter are my most vivid memories of flying, that's not such a bad track record considering the millions of miles that I've flown – to Australia and back ten times, to the United States, South Africa, all over Europe. In the end, I have to side with Bobby and say that it *is* the safest way to travel.

✳✳✳✳

If there's one kind of flying I don't mind at all, it's cruising down to Rio in long silver boots. Perhaps I had better explain.

I was filming a television show in Germany, and the song they wanted me to do was *Flying Down to Rio* – an old Thirties musical num-ber ('Rio, Rio by the sea-o', if you recall). They'd built an old biplane set for me to sit in, and I was done up in a marvellous little silver Amy Johnson hat, with goggles, blonde wig, and an incredible pair of specially made silver boots (the Germans are very thorough).

I got into the plane, and then I realized that the director hadn't been

78

so clever after all because the cameras could only see just below my neck. I called out to Irving Davies, my choreographer:

'Look,' I said, 'I've got a fortune on my feet but no-one can see them. Do you think I could fly this plane down to Rio with one leg out the side?'

'Of course, darling,' he said.

So that was how we did the song. It was lovely. I wish I could fly everywhere like that – preferably without leaving the ground!

DORIS'S GIRL

'People see you on-stage looking all glamorous and they think, ooh, I wish I could be a star. They should come backstage and see worrits really like!'

Ome of the best things about being a success is that it gives you a certain power to make things happen. I didn't realize I had this power, or any power at all, until one day at the London Palladium.

Audrey Jeans came into my dressing room, which was meant to be the second dressing room in the theatre. She looked around and said: 'This is a disgrace. You must get them to decorate it for you.'

It looked all right to me. I even thought it was quite comfortable. 'I don't mind it,' I said

to her. I was happy to take things as I found them.

She gave me a pained look. 'Well, I wouldn't have it,' she said.

All right, I thought. Audrey wants to give me some advice; why not take it. I said so to Bobby, and he agreed, so he went along to see Jack Matthews, the stage manager, who was a lovely man and always very good to us.

'Jack,' he said. 'I want Cilla's dressing room painted. It's in a terrible state.'

'Is it?' said Jack. 'OK. I'll send someone round.'

That was it. No arguing. Next thing, a feller came round. 'What colour do you want?'

This was going a bit fast for us. 'Er, er, er . . . white?' we said.

'OK,' said the feller, and it was done for the weekend. That was when it dawned on me that if you're a success in show business you can ask for things *and* get them.

Things were looking up. A few years later I was the first performer to get a loo put in at the Palladium. Not only that, I had a shower as well, and for the first time the star dressing room lived up to its name.

If you think of all the stars who have played there, especially for the Royal Command Performances, it does seem amazing that it took until the 1970s to bring the plumbing arrangements into the twentieth century; but that is often the way with the old theatres in the city centres. They have their special place in history, and are wonderful venues to play, but the latest generation of concert halls and arts centres completely outdoes them when it comes to facilities.

At the Palladium, the old loo was next-door to the star dressing-room. Unfortunately, it wasn't a Ladies. It was the Artistes' loo, and you had to queue in the corridor with the men if you wanted to spend a penny.

Because we already knew the Palladium, this time we made it part of our original negotiations with the management that I should have a loo and a shower in my dressing room. Bobby went to a meeting with Louis Benjamin, who was in charge of the theatre, and put in the request.

'All right,' said Louis Benjamin, agreeing immediately.

'Eh?' said Bobby, who'd been expecting he'd have to argue it. 'How come that was so easy?'

'No-one's ever asked before,' came the reply.

It was as simple as that. We only had to ask. At the same time, I doubt we would have had our way if we hadn't had the right bargaining power.

Ken Dodd was especially pleased. He followed me into the Palladium and into some other theatres where I also insisted on having my own private facilities. He sent me a telegram of congratulations – and addressed it to 'The Queen of the Loos'!

Since that time, one or two other stars have played the Palladium in *real* style. Yul Brynner, for instance, had a personal suite installed when he was there for *The King and I,* and later he took it on tour with him to the States – all his own personal pieces of furniture, everything he needed to make his life backstage as comfortable as possible.

Some managements aren't nearly so accommodating. They can't see the sense in bothering to look after performers, often because they have such a low opinion of them. Worst of all are the small-town places where the venue isn't a proper theatre but, say, the town hall. There have been times when I felt like inviting the whole audience backstage to visit some of the broom cupboards I have been offered as a dressing room. I'm sure it would have cured a few false impressions about the 100 per cent glamorous life we are supposed to lead.

Once in Scotland the facilities were so dreadful I checked into a hotel for the afternoon. The venue was a town hall; backstage it was dark and dingy, and all you had to sit on were long green leatherette benches – like you were waiting to go on trial. I said no thank you, went to the hotel, changed there, and came back to the theatre in full make-up.

I said to the audience: 'I don't think I've been here before. Tell me, what is this place?'

Someone shouted out: 'A dump.'

I said: 'I'm glad *you* said that!'

There was a big fuss in the papers, and they all agreed it was a disgrace to expect visiting artistes to put up with such terrible conditions. I got a letter of apology' from the mayor, and the last thing I heard they were promising to spend £20,000 on improvements. That's not a lot these days, but at least it would be a start.

❋❋❋❋

Then there is what the advertising people call your Recognition Factor, or how many people actually know who you are and can get your name right. I usually do well on that score, partly because there aren't nearly so many women as men at the top of the bill in show business. But I quickly learnt that the picture of me in other people's minds is never the same, and it's also very different from the 'real' me that I see in the mirror.

I shouldn't be surprised. Years ago, it used to throw people that I could be in a room with them at the same time as I was appearing before their very eyes on television. And in a different frock!

Bobby's Dad said to me one Saturday: 'You're on *Juke Box Jury* tonight.'

I said: 'I know.'

'Well,' he said, 'shouldn't you be getting down there?'

I explained that this was the recorded show. They made two programmes on the same day, and one was shown live and the other one was kept for the following Saturday. He still looked puzzled, and when the show came on and we all watched it together he was even more puzzled, and kept looking across from the Screen Me to the Real Me, and back, and back again. It was like someone rubbing their eyes to test if they were seeing double.

This kind of thing went on for quite a while. He'd say to me: 'You were on television the other night. Do you know what you did?'

Then he'd tell me what the programme was called, who I was on with, what I said, then what so-and-so said – just as if I hadn't been there at all! I suppose that's what people used to call 'the magic of television'. Today, what with all the videos and other equipment they can have, people are more sophisticated. But twenty years ago it may have seemed like magic the way a person could be seen and heard on millions of little boxes all over the country, and seconds later that same person drives past in their car – Eh? What's that? How did she do that? Even Bobby himself was bewildered by it at first, as he will tell you.

Bobby: 'We were down in Wales for Cilla's first television programme, called *Discs A-Gogo*. Kent Walton was on it. They used to record programmes on about the Wednesday and show them on Saturday. I was standing in the studio watching a monitor and Cilla came on. She smiled. I thought: "She's smiling at me." So I smiled back – at this monitor! Then I turned round – and there was Cilla, with her back to me. I thought: "That's funny. First she's here, then she's there." Then it clicked, and I said to myself: "You daft wallie!" But it *was* odd at first, until you got the hang of all those simultaneous images flashing at you from all corners of the studio.'

Face-to-face meetings, on the other hand, can be completely matter- of-fact. If there's a bunch of fellers working on a building site, or mending the road, and I walk past, they think it's perfectly natural that I should be there and so they call out something like 'Ey, Cilla. Great show,' and carry on working. I have even been taken for granted in far-flung places like Singapore. Several people there recognized me but simply said hello. They had no trouble in accepting that I was in Singapore, just like them, and treated it as a perfectly normal situation.

Somehow I have always had an image of being approachable, and people don't feel inhibited about coming up for a quick chat or to ask for an autograph. On the whole, that is the image I am happiest with. Just once in a while, though, I like to dress up and *be* the star, like at a premiere, and then of course I wouldn't want a lot of people coming up to me because that would take away from the specialness of the occasion.

So, most of the time, my image is not particularly romantic, and no- one has ever flung himself down at my feet. Except once.

I was talking on the radio about Shirley Bassey, and saying how she came across as untouchable. If you walked into a room and saw her there, you might gasp and whisper 'Aaah! There's Shirley Bassey', but you really wouldn't do anything about it. Men do go mad about her, though, and dream of flinging themselves at her feet. No-one wants to do that with me, I said to the interviewer. Well, no sooner had I got out of the studio and onto the street than this feller rushed up, threw himself on the pavement and started kissing my feet! He must have heard the programme on his car radio and then spotted me leaving the BBC.

Suddenly there he was, slobbering over my shoes like a big puppy. It wasn't all that great, really; a bit kinky, even. In fact, I wished I hadn't opened my mouth. So much for romance!

For my *Cilla* programme I did an item in a Green Shield stamps shop. I put on an overall like the other girls, and served on the counter. The idea was to do a kind of *Candid Camera* piece, with a hidden camera recording the customers' reactions to being served by me.

A girl came in with a big pile of books which she wanted to exchange for about nine things in the catalogue. I fetched eight of them for her, then I kept getting the ninth one wrong – deliberately, so as to wind her up a little and push her into saying something for our film.

I could get nothing. She was the soul of patience. The last article on her list was a Morphy-Richards iron, so I brought her a garden hose – no, an iron; then a toaster – no, an iron; then a table lamp – no, an iron; then a hairbrush – no, an iron . . . In the end I got exasperated. I said to her: 'Do you know who I am?'

'Yeah,' she said, 'you're Cilla Black. How long have you been working here?'

We had a similar spot in a supermarket, with me working in a white coat.

'Hello, love,' I said to this nice old lady.

'Oh, hello, love,' she said.

'Do you know who I am?' I asked.

The old lady thought for a bit, then she pulled at her chin. 'Wait a minute,' she said, 'let me just think . . .'

'Shall I give you a clue?' I said a few seconds later, when she didn't come up with a name.

'Oh, all right, love. Yes,' she said.

'My surname's Black,' I said.

She looked at me, then her eyes went all bright. 'Yeeees!' she said. 'You're Doris's girl. How are you keeping, love?' And she gave me a lovely smile.

'No, I'm not,' I said.

'Yes,' she insisted. 'You're Doris's girl. How's your Mum?'

This went on for quite a long time, and it made a lovely film. Unfortunately, we were never able to show it because the lady wouldn't sign the authority which we have to get from members of the public. It turned out she was living in a Home and didn't want to offend the people there. I can't think she would have for one moment, but that was her wish and we had to respect it. Another one for the cutting-room floor!

✳✳✳✳

The other nice part of being famous is that lots of people make a fuss of you, and that's usually very pleasant. Not that you should expect preferential treatment, because there are enough other people around who take the attitude 'I don't care who she is, she'd better not try and put one over on me.' It's not the public who think this so much as people in official positions – like the woman in Customs at the airport.

We'd just come back from Ireland, and while Bobby was waiting for the luggage I said I'd walk straight through and make sure Tom, our driver, was there with the car. I went through the Green section, carrying just my handbag. There was a woman Customs officer in there and she called me over and asked where I'd been. I told her, so then she wanted to look through my handbag. I thought this was all a bit unnecessary. After all, what would I be smuggling in from Ireland in a handbag? Still, I gave her the bag and let her search it. When she'd done that she said:

'Will you take your fur coat off.'

'No,' I said. 'I won't. I'm freezing already.'

She gave me one of those blank stares. 'Where did you buy it?' she wanted to know.

'In Liverpool.'

'Have you got the receipt for it?'

'No,' I said. 'I don't go around carrying receipts for everything I've got with me.'

This woman and I were running out of things to say to each other, but she didn't want to let me go that easily. It was all so stupid and petty. Then Bobby came along with one of the other fellers in our party. I explained I was still in the Customs hall because this woman wanted me to take my fur coat off.

So Bobby said: 'All right, take it off. She won't wear it.'

I took it off and laid it on the counter. 'Right,' said Bobby to the woman, 'the coat's off. Now what do you want to do?'

'Er, er, that's all right,' said the woman, suddenly embarrassed. 'You can put it on again now.'

So I did, and we left. But I did think: there must be better ways of doing a job like hers. On the other hand, since we're talking about Customs officials, I have to admit that once or twice – at least – I have been glad of their kindness and understanding.

Coming back after our first trip to the States, Bobby and I went to the Duty-free shop to buy some presents for the girls in the office as a thank-you for fixing up our trip and making it run nice and smoothly. We chose some trinkets and small bits and pieces, nothing expensive, and it was all put in a carrier bag.

We went through Customs, and the feller asked if I had anything to declare. I said no.

'What's in that bag?' he asked, pointing to the carrier.

'Oh, that's alright,' I said. 'I've bought all that at the Duty-free shop.'

Well, nobody told me you couldn't buy as much as you liked in there and never pay duty on it! But the feller was kind. He just raised his eyes to heaven and said:

'Oh dear. Go on, then.'

We were coming back from the Canary Islands another time, and I'd bought this lovely big leather and suede handbag. I'd actually been using it while we were out there, so I had it on my arm when we came through Customs.

'Have you anything to declare?' asked the feller.

'No,' I said.

In those days they used to put chalk signs on everything they passed. So the feller reached for my bag with his chalk.

'Don't put chalk on that,' I said to him. 'I've only just bought it.'

Again I got the weary look and the eyes raised to heaven. Then he said: 'Dear God!' And to me: 'All right. Off you go.'

Me Through the Ages, or, Only the Clothes and Hair are Different. The pictures are in date order, from left to right, top to bottom, and start with 1963, just after I'd left the office to be a singer. Then it all gets more swinging – skirts are shorter and so is the hair. By 1970 Bobby and I look like one half of Abba, and in the studio shot I am six months pregnant with Robert, but you can't really tell, can you? Then come hot pants and long hair, then the hair goes shorter again through the Seventies. (Today it's as you see it on the front cover of this book.)

Going back to the business of being recognized in public, I had a really daft encounter in what I'll call a well-known London store. I chose several things in this department, and the assistant asked me for my autograph which I gave her. When it came to paying, I wrote out a cheque which had 'CILLA BLACK' on it and handed it to her.

Almost without looking at the cheque, she said: 'Have you any form of identification?'

That mystified me for a couple of seconds, then I said: 'You've got my autograph.'

'Oh,' she said, 'that's not what I meant. I have to have some official form of identification.'

I said: 'I just signed that piece of paper for you. That's who I am.'

'I'm afraid I can't accept this cheque,' she replied, 'unless you can prove you're Cilla Black.'

She was obviously playing this by the book. Privately she had accepted my autograph, so she didn't really need to be further convinced that I was Cilla Black. However, the staff manual must have said you had to get written identification from the customer if they paid by cheque. So there we were. Stuck again, like at the airport, except that I didn't have to hang around the store if I didn't Want to.

By now a crowd was gathering with other people wanting my autograph. This is something that happens. It only takes one person to recognize you and come up and ask for an autograph, then you're stopped. While you're signing, other people are going past thinking: 'What's this? Why does she want her autograph? Oh, it's Cilla Black. I'll have one as well.' Before you know what's happening, a queue has formed.

So, next thing, I was signing my name for a line of people who, like the assistant, thought I was Cilla Black but, unlike the assistant, didn't need written proof. It was crazy, but it's just one of those topsy-turvy things. The assistant was making a fuss over goods worth about forty pounds, whereas I could have gone to a jewellers down the road and bought a diamond bracelet for twenty-five thousand pounds without even writing my address on the back of the cheque. That has actually happened, so no wonder I get confused at times!

On another occasion Bobby wanted to buy me some pearls. We went along to the jewellers and looked at them, but I wasn't sure if they were right for me.

The assistant said: 'Why don't you take them home with you and see how you like them after a few days.'

I said: 'Well, that's a nice idea but we're going on holiday.'

She said: 'Take them with you.'

So I did. They didn't ask for a deposit or anything. Mind you, it was clever salesmanship because she was counting on the fact that after keeping the pearls for a fortnight I would be more inclined to have them than give them back – and that's what in fact happened. But, to go back to the original point, would she have made the offer if I hadn't been someone she recognized? Probably not. Even so, how is it that she could recognize me on behalf of the jewellers and yet the girl in the forty-quid shop couldn't? Experience, probably. After all, the first girl could have settled it by going to see her supervisor.

Being Cilla Black does have its little difficulties. All the same, if I had to choose, I'd rather be her than Doris's girl!

THE
CUTTING-ROOM
FLOOR

'Doing Surprise Surprise *is a lot of fun, but it makes
your heart go a bit because you never know what
the people will look like or what they'll say. Rehearsals are like doing a show by braille.'*

Sometimes I think to myself: 'What am I rehearsing this for? It could turn out completely different.' Very often it does, but the funny
thing is, the show seems to work *because* it has
that exciting ingredient of no-one being quite in
charge of what's going on.

Our relationship with the viewers is a special one. At first we had no idea of the impact
that we were having on the public. Then, one
evening, Christopher Biggins and I had some
time off from making *Surprise Surprise* and we
decided to go and see Alan Bennett's play, *Forty*

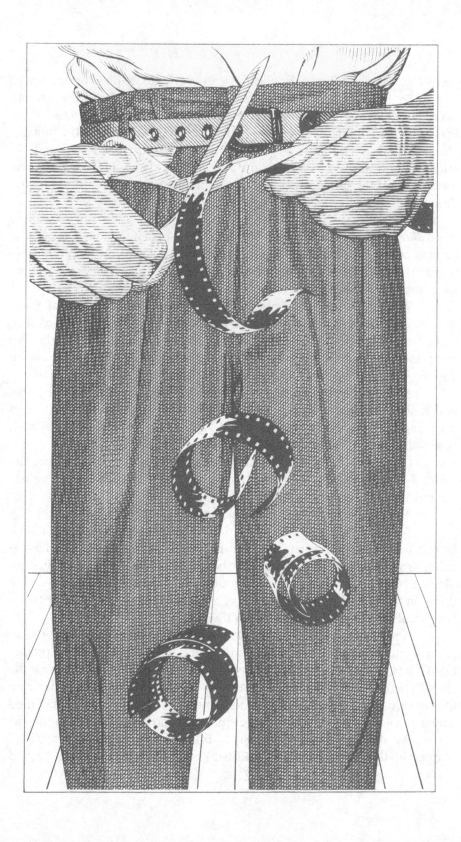

Years On. We walked into the theatre, and everyone in the foyer scattered!

We found it amazing that the sight of the two of us together should make people so nervous. Did they really think we were trying to set them up for the programme? It seemed incredible to us and yet, had I thought about it, there *is* a difference between the people who make up the studio audience and write in for tickets and actually hope we will have a surprise for them, and the others who don't write in and are maybe terrified by the thought of appearing on the show.

I know that some people have good reason to be shy. Once, for the *Cilla* programme, we went live to a block of flats where we had the camera and microphone mounted in a big crane. I said: 'Now, if you recognize these flats as being where you live, come to the balcony and give us a wave and you'll be on television.'

We had a terrific response. The camera lights went on, and all these front doors opened and people came pouring out onto the balconies. The crane went up and down, then moved in close to film people outside their front doors and then I interviewed them from the studio. This went on for a while, then I saw another likely couple and said: 'Right. We'll go in there.'

As the camera moved towards their balcony, the feller broke away and rushed indoors, leaving the girl outside. I asked her if she'd been watching the show. She said yes, so I said: 'Well, what's going on with him? What's he run in for? He should be out here with you.'

I shouted after the feller and coaxed him until he came out again, which he did and gave the camera a wave. There was a younger girl on the balcony as well, so I said: 'Who's this?'

'She's the babysitter,' came the reply.

Why have a babysitter when there are two adults watching television? I wondered to myself. It later turned out that the feller was having an affair with the woman, and her husband, who thought his wife was out playing bingo, was sitting in a pub round the corner watching the whole thing on television! It led to a divorce, and I was a little sad to hear that – but people do bring these things on themselves.

A similar scandal blew up after an episode of *Surprise Surprise*. A feller wrote in to tell us about his fiancée, and what a marvellous tapdancer she was. Could we surprise her with a phone-call and invite her on the show? Then we found out from our records that the girl had written in during the previous series to tell us about her fiancé, saying that he was a talented singer. Could I phone him up and surprise him and invite him on the show?

We thought it would be fun to link the two items together. So I phoned up the girl and did the surprise on her. 'Where's your feller?' I asked her. I told her that he'd written me a letter about her and that they were both going to be on the show. Then I spoke to the feller and explained that she'd said he was a good singer. 'Oh,' he said, 'I'll bloody well kill 'er.'

So we had them both on the show. He sang *42nd Street* dressed in top hat and tails and she did some tapdancing, and it made a lovely piece for the programme. As extra surprises we had the Roly Polys to dance for us, and Biggins was one of the Roly Polys. It all went off extremely well.

Two days later I saw this headline in the paper: 'SURPRISE SUR-PRISE – IT'S MY ?**!??! HUSBAND'. I read on, and found that this guy, who not only owed his wife £3,000 in maintenance, had gone on television with the other woman!

Some people do leave me a little bit flabbergasted. I mean, did he really think he'd get away with it unnoticed on a programme watched by fifteen million viewers? Even if his own wife hadn't seen him someone else who knew him was bound to. It did strike me as a little, well, tactless.

Not that we can't be surprised ourselves. On the *Cilla* show some years ago I was knocking on doors to see if people were watching the show – and I ended up in a brothel. The door was opened by a woman. She said yes, she'd been watching the programme with her friend. I thought she looked a bit rough but I wasn't very quick on the uptake. In the hall-way was a line of men. Still it didn't click. I just thought: 'She's got a lot of friends.' Then the camera lens steamed up! In those days it was still fairly rare to film in this very mobile way, and the crew hadn't allowed for the humidity in the house after coming in from outdoors. I was peering through this cloudy picture from the studio and a feller came up on the screen.

'Who are you?' I asked him. He gave me a name and I said: 'Well, you've gorrer nice tan.' He did too – he was a coloured feller! I was just going to ask him where he'd been on holiday when I realized, and swal-lowed the question.

After the programme, we got a lot of stick from viewers. 'Of all the streets to pick, Cilla, why did you have to go into a red-light district?' – that kind of thing. I couldn't really say why we picked that one, but I don't mind putting some of the blame on a certain football club. The rea-son is that we had to share cameras with *Match of the Day,* so wherever they were filming, we were restricted to that area of the country. Come to think of it, if our cameramen had stayed in that house much longer, *we'd* have been Match of the Day!

So much for the gaffes which sometimes slip through the net and then are seen by millions of viewers. If you only knew how many other items we cancel or have to edit out of the final show.

One recent non-starter had promised to be one of the most romantic items we had ever screened. A boy aged twenty-one – we'll call him Colin – wrote to tell us that he and his girlfriend were getting engaged at Christmastime and he thought it would be a lovely surprise if he could propose to her on the show.

Nice one, we thought. Then someone in the team suggested that Colin should make a date with his girl so she'd think he was coming to take her out. On the Outside Broadcasting camera we'd have Toni Arthur knocking on the door.

Came the day, and Toni knocked on the door. The girl opened it, saw Toni and the camera crew – and immediately slammed it shut. Behind the door we could hear all sorts of noises, swearing and other kerfuffle, then it opened again. This time Toni managed to persuade the girl to come to the studio because her boyfriend was there and she could see the show and get a nice surprise. We had a white Rolls-Royce to take her there and that was fine. She came on the show and I said to her:

'Do you know why you're here?'

She said: 'No.'

I said: 'Well, I'll tell you. But first of all, can we have some soft lights and romantic music.'

The band started to play something gentle, with lots of strings. Colin was sat there in a dinner jacket, and in one of his pockets was the ring we'd bought for him to give to her. I said to him:

'Right, Colin. Off you go.'

He stood up and walked over to his girl, got down on one knee, just as we'd rehearsed it, gave her the ring and said: 'Will you . . . .'

That was as far as he got because she interrupted him with a loud: 'No!'

The audience roared. I quickly said to the girl: 'Now, don't worry. I know this is all a bit daunting and embarrassing, I can quite understand that. But, really, in the privacy of your own home, or in some more suitable setting, I'm sure you'd say yes, wouldn't you?'

She said: 'No!'

Now I was struggling, but I carried on. I explained that we had arranged for them to be taken out in the white Rolls-Royce to have dinner at a wonderful Italian restaurant. 'I'm sure,' I said, 'that when you've had a lovely meal, and you're in a romantic mood, and he asks you again, you'll say . . .'

'No!' she said, just as firmly as before.

I was more than a bit exasperated by all this non-cooperation. If I'd been her, I'd have said yes just to get off the set.

'Right,' I said, 'you can give us our ring back! *And* you're not going out to dinner!'

Afterwards, everyone in the studio agreed that we'd have to cut the item. It was great television, but we only wanted to give surprises to people who accepted them. All that 'No, No, No' certainly made a change but it was against programme policy, so we dropped it. Later we had an angry letter from, of all people, Colin's mum! Why had we cut out her Colin? she demanded. It really is amazing what some people will put up with in order to be famous for five minutes.

Someone thought up a marvellous piece of revenge on the girl-friend. We'd keep the item going as a continuation piece, and each week we'd bring the girl a different feller. I'd say to her: 'Will this one do?' She'd say: 'No!' – and we'd keep it going until she gave in. Everyone on the show thought it was such a great idea, we'd better keep it to ourselves. So we never did anything about it. CUT!

Reunions always go down well with the audience, and some of the scenes are really quite moving. I am fairly hardened to it now, but in the first two series Biggins never was. I always knew if a story had a good emotional pull because I'd hear Biggins whimpering off-camera.

Our researchers came up with a promising story involving a man in his seventies who hadn't seen his daughter since she was one year old. Now she had grandchildren of her own. It took the researchers a long time to track her down, and then they were able to pass on the good news to the man.

'That's great,' he said. 'I'm really looking forward to meeting her.'

'Right,' we said. 'We'll fix a day for it, and then we'll bring you along to the studio. . .'

'What do you mean, studio?' he asked.

'For the filming,' we said.

'Oh, no,' he said. 'I'll be very happy to meet my daughter again after all these years. But I'm certainly not going to do it on television!'

CUT!

We had what we thought was a lovely item about a fireman who had done voluntary service for thirty-three years. Not only that, he had raised thousands of pounds for the fire service charity. Of all the many rescues he had taken part in, the most unusual was when he had to save a pig *and* give it the kiss of life.

The pig survived, so did the fireman, and now we had him and the pig's grandson in the studio. The idea was to ask this feller to show us how he had brought the original pig back to life, but just when he was about to start the kiss of life, we'd say:

'That's all right. You don't have to blow into that one. Blow into this.'

Then we'd hand him this balloon pig which we'd had made to order for £150. We never got that far. The grandson pig was impossible. Elephants you can train; camels you can train; any animal fit for the circus can be trained to perform in front of an audience. But this pig was terrified and couldn't be calmed down. It was dragged on the set wearing a harness and squealing blue murder.

Its handler had assured us there'd be no problem. 'He'll be fine,' he said. 'He's been in shows,' he said. 'He's used to seeing a lot of people.'

Unfortunately, the pig must have had a short memory, because he made such a noise he completely destroyed the item. In no time at all I was put right off doing it, and even if we had gone ahead with filming we could never have shown it because the RSPCA and the animal rights people would have jumped on us. There was only one thing for it. CUT!

I went into a garage to do a request item – a bit like a Cillagram. 'Right,' I said, 'does anybody have a message they'd like to send, 'cos you're on the telly now.'

This feller came forward. Extremely camp, he was. He gazed at the camera, all misty: 'I want to send all my love, and would you please sing *You're My World*.'

'Fine,' I said, 'I'll do that. But who's it for?'

He looked straight at the camera and said, softly but intensely: '*He'll* know who it's for.'

Do you know, we couldn't use that either. Too passionate for us – and besides, we're a family show. CUT!

****

One Christmas the BBC flew me in a private jet to Belfast – all very hush-hush-to do a special show live from an aircraft hangar. Frankie Howerd was on the show, and The Bachelors, and one of the main items was a series of televised reunions between members of the armed forces and the wives and families they were separated from that Christmas.

Technically it was a very ambitious project – the first live 'reverse colour' broadcast, which meant that the couples would be able to see each other as they talked, rather than just being seen speaking to a camera. As for me, I would be singing in Belfast to an orchestra that was playing in the studio in Shepherds Bush. On top of that, we had a link-up with a choir in Wales. When it was all over, the film was earmarked for the BBC archives.

It was a great show, immediate and moving. The troops came in straight from patrol duty and sat down, shoved their loaded rifles under the seats and watched the show. When we did the reunions, people got very emotional and the tears were flowing like the River Mersey. One wife, I remember especially well, stood there in London holding her baby and looking at her husband in Belfast and she was so choked she couldn't utter a single word.

As soon as the show was over, we were off and in the air about two minutes later. The security throughout had been so tight that even the flowers in the hangar had to be screened for explosives. Nothing, luckily, happened to alarm anyone on the airfield itself, but I did hear a funny story about the rehearsal pianist. He was down to play in a singalong with me and the troops before the show started. He was being driven through Belfast in an armoured car, when they had to stop because of a puncture.

'Suddenly all the others jumped out,' he told me a little while later. He was still shaking. 'They rushed to cover the street corners. Kids started throwing bricks at us. Then the police arrived. I sat inside the vehicle thinking: "Why me? I've only come here to play a few songs!".'

I don't think he ever quite got used to Belfast. More happily, the show was rated a big success, and on the Monday we had a phone call from Billy Cotton.

'Wonderful show,' he said. 'Come to lunch on Wednesday and we'll get the champagne out and watch the replay.'

'Fine,' we said, but a little while later he rang back.

'I've got a terrible admission to make,' he said. 'They've wiped the whole show.'

Apparently, some genius at the BBC had noticed that a piece of paper hadn't been signed to say the show could be seen overseas. So they erased the whole thing. So much for the archives, posterity and all that. We didn't get our lunch, either.

****

Then there was the case of The Black Man Who Never Was. We found out that Muhammad Ali was coming over to fight at the Albert Hall. This was early in his career and he hadn't seen the Albert Hall, so I was going to take him, live on the *Cilla* show, to the hall and say to him:

'This is where you're going to be fighting two weeks from now.'

We also knew there'd be an audience in the hall, listening to a classical radio concert that was going out all over Europe. The way we planned it, he would make an entrance high up in the auditorium and then walk down those trillions of steep stairs to the floor. It would have looked incredible, because in those days he was in his prime, a real Adonis. The audience would have gone wild.

Then he got 'flu and had to cancel. That was a drag, but all was not lost. Also in the show we had an 'Unusual Ambitions' spot, an early version of the *Jim 'll Fix It* show, and at that time we'd just heard from a guy who did a marvellous impression of Al Jolson. He wrote to say that he gave lots of performances for charity but his dearest ambition was to sing on television, and could he sing on our show.

We thought: 'Why don't we take him and let him sing at the Albert Hall?'

So it was agreed. We didn't tell him beforehand, it was a bit like doing a 'Surprise' on him. He came on-stage, all blacked up as Al Jolson, and I said to him:

'Not only are you going to sing on television in front of twenty million viewers, but the whole of Europe is going to hear you tonight because you're going to sing at the Royal – Albert – Hall!'

'Great!' he said. 'Oh! Marvellous!'

He seemed really excited at the prospect. Then he and I went out of the studio, climbed into the chauffeur-driven car which was discreetly miked up, and set off for the Albert Hall. This feller was incredible. He just couldn't believe what was going on. As we sat on the back seat he said to me:

'Where are we really going?'

'We're going to the Royal Albert Hall,' I said, 'and you're going to sing *Mammy* to twenty million viewers at home and to heaven knows how many people all over Europe.'

Well, he thought about all that for a few seconds, then he turned to me and said:

'Don't worry, Cilla. I won't let you down.'

He certainly didn't. He was a real little pro the way he sang to all those classical music fans in the audience. He did us proud. In fact, a friend of mine, Tommy Nutter, happened to be there, and he said it was the best thing he either saw or heard all evening. It was only afterwards that we realized how, quite by chance, Muhammad Ali had been unable to appear, so we'd sent on as his stand-in an English feller blacked up with white painted lips and a negro wig. If the story had got out, we could have had the Race Relations Board down on us!

Two reasons why I needed a proper house to live in, rather than a West End flat, were our first two French Briards, Ada (left) and Sophie. Sophie came to us after I saw her on Blue Peter where she was being featured as part of the first litter to be born in this country. It was my birthday, and we phoned up the breeder, Mrs Trueman, and bought her. After a while she started pining for company and we got Ada. Later Mrs Trueman showed them for us and Ada won the title Best of Rare Breeds at Crufts's. When we bred from them, Ada and Sophie both had a litter within days of each other, so then we had fourteen little puppies snuffling round the place. Ada had eight pups, and we named them after characters in Shakespeare – Hamlet, Julius, Othello, Desdemona, Romeo, Juliet, Cleo and Cymbeline. Sophie's six were named after Liverpool districts- Dingle, Kirkdale, Gateacre, Allerton, Garston and Anfield. If it had been my choice alone, one of Sophie's pups might have been called Everton, because on my side of the family the men are Evertonians. But Bobby looked so upset when I suggested it, I didn't have the heart to insist.

With Bobby and Robert not long after we'd moved into the house in Denham. The three woolly figures are, left to right, Sophie, Ada and Walter. Walter was a lovely dog but so short-sighted we should have called him Magoo. He kept bumping into things, and even our chickens could pinch bits off his dinner plate without him noticing.

A PLACE
OF OUR OWN

'We kept having houses surveyed, all by the same feller. "We want that," we'd say to him. "Don't bother," he said. "It's slipping down the hill." Time after time this happened. "No, not that one. It's rotting to pieces." Sixteen years ago, we were looking at £70,000 slums.'

I was getting desperate. I was imminent with Robert, but we had nowhere suitable to live. We weren't exactly on the streets because we had a big luxurious flat in Portland Place, with three large bedrooms, an enormous lounge, two bathrooms, garages underneath – for what it was, it was fine, but I thought: 'I can't bring a baby into this flat, plus a nanny and two dogs.'

In the early part of the pregnancy it wasn't too bad, but when the realities began to close in I found myself going frantic over the idea of living there with a baby. There was no open space,

and when you did go out the streets were crowded with people and traffic, not to mention the pollution from the car exhausts. Indoors, as well, you never get the same peace and privacy in a flat that you can have in your own house.

About a fortnight before Robert was born, the weather was very hot and I was having difficulty sleeping, which is fairly normal when you're that pregnant. But one night it wasn't so much being pregnant as the noise from a neighbouring flat that was driving me mad.

Every few minutes they were playing Michael Jackson singing *ABC.* Over and over again, this virginal voice came squeaking through the wall. Now, much as I loved Michael Jackson (or all 5 of them), I didn't need this at three o'clock in the morning when I was eight and a half months pregnant.

I said to Bobby: 'You'll have to go next door and tell them to turn their records down.'

Bobby said: 'Oh, I can't do that.' Besides, it wasn't bothering him like it was getting to me.

'Well,' I said, 'if you won't go, I will.'

I was really upset about it. The neighbours knew I was pregnant, so why did they do this. I was feeling truly sorry for myself as I walked through our kitchen. The door opened on to a balcony which we shared with the flat next door. The neighbours on that side must have been diplomats or some kind of government officials. I'm not really sure what they did, but they were big on entertaining.

I reached the back door of the other flat and marched in. I had my finger ready to wag at them, and I'd got as far as: 'Don't you realize . . .' when I stopped.

The place was full of black Americans, all beaming at me and happily grooving to soul music. Then a lady came up to me. 'Oh, Cilla!' she said. 'Come on in. Woncha have a drink.'

Bobby never saw me till eight o'clock that morning. (Not that he came looking for me.) But when I saw all those happy people I didn't have the heart to tell them to turn their records down. And once I knew I couldn't beat them, it wasn't hard to join them instead.

When I finally did get home, I thought: 'Well, that was alright. But I can't go on doing it. We'll have to move – but where?'

We had been looking at properties for some while, and we'd had a lot of letdowns, either because the surveys were bad or because some people get funny ideas when it comes to selling their property. There was a lovely house in Hampstead which I wanted as soon as I saw it. We travelled all the way down from Blackpool at the weekend to see it – I was in a summer show and couldn't go during the week. When we got there, a woman showed us round and then, after we'd said how much we liked it, told us it was already under offer. What's more, it was under offer to someone we knew. This woman must have been a bit starstruck, that's all I can think. She had us come down all the way from Blackpool just so she could meet someone she'd seen on the telly. I was a bit upset about that.

Then one day I was going through the property columns in the *Sunday Times* and I came across a house in Denham, set in its own grounds of seventeen acres. I remembered Denham, because we had been to look at a property nearby in Chalfont St Peter. I thought to myself: 'Ooh, I'd like to see that.'

Bobby was in the Harley Street Clinic having his wisdom teeth out, so I made all the arrangements through the office and on the Friday Bobby came out of hospital and we went down to Denham. We found the road and drove up by the golf course until we came to the entrance and saw the nameplate for the house. We turned in. It was the middle of summer, lots of flowers were out and everything looked very colourful and pretty. Next thing we saw was an attractive red-brick house.

'That looks really nice,' I said to Bobby. Perhaps this time we would strike lucky. I began to feel optimistic.

Then the car turned a corner in the driveway which took us away from the red-brick house. Seconds later we found ourselves looking at the front of a really big house which had been hidden by some trees.

'Eh?' said Bobby, 'that's a bit much. I thought ours was meant to be set in its own grounds. But that's two houses we've seen already.'

'I don't know,' I said, mystified. Then I remembered that the house we were going to see had a cottage in the grounds. That must have been the red-brick house we had seen – and mistaken for the main house!

Well, after that our mouths opened wider and wider as we met the owners and they showed us round their magnificent home with its beautiful gardens and grounds. I knew immediately that I wanted it. On the Saturday we got in touch with our surveyor and asked him to go to Denham and survey it.

He didn't mess about. 'I know that house,' he said. 'Get it!'

We needed no further encouragement. The house was under offer to us by the Sunday, and the sale went through. The people we bought it from wanted a quick sale anyway, because they'd already bought themselves a smaller house, and I think they were glad to find a buyer who didn't hum and hah and try to niggle over a few bob. In fact, they told us that somebody had been trying to do just that. The owner wasn't happy about it because he felt he'd priced the house realistically for a quick sale. So they'd been going back and forth like that without really getting anywhere – when along we came, paid the asking price and got the house.

****

It took a while to settle in. In fact, it was a bit like arriving in a frontier town in the Old West. Before we could relax and enjoy the place, first we had to fight a boundary war with the neighbours.

We'd only been in the house a few days when we noticed that Ada and Sophie, our Briards, kept coming indoors with bits of barbed wire stuck in the long fur at the back of their legs. Bobby thought they'd been in our woods at the bottom of the paddock, so one Sunday afternoon he went down there to have a look. I'll let him tell the rest of this story.

Bobby: 'I walked down to the woods and found a feller hammering away at a post. Next to him were some more posts and a big coil of barbed wire. On our land!

"What are you doing?" I asked him.

"I'm putting this fence up," he said.

"It's not your land," I said to him.

"Well it's not yours," he replied.

"Oh yes it is," I said.

I could hardly believe it. I looked around at what he had been doing. He was a neighbour who lived on the other side of our woods, and he and another neighbour were quite openly extending their gardens into our property. It was more than just an extension: if he'd gone on and finished the job he'd have doubled the length of his garden.

"No," I heard him telling me. "you've got it all wrong. We've always used this land. Besides, we've been here for years and you've only been here for five minutes. And the previous owners said it wasn't theirs."

"I don't care what the previous owners said," I told him. "This is my property and I want you to get off it."

"No," he said, "I won't."

I wasn't going to argue with him. I went and phoned the local police, who came down and had a word with the feller, who by now had his mate with him who'd also been helping himself to a piece of our property. After he'd had a talk with the policeman, he agreed to leave. Then he pointed to me and said:

"But I'm not going while he's still standing there."

106

Me! I only owned the place, and this feller's trying to order me off it. Granted, I may have been a bit sharp with him, but I felt I had good reason. Anyway, I said I'd go back to the house with the policeman if the neighbour made sure he got out of my woods. We were walking up through the paddock when the policeman said:

"You know, really we had no authority here because it's a domestic matter."

"What do you mean?" I asked him. "If you can't do anything about people coming in and stealing land, who can?"

"Well," he said. "*You* can. In a case like this, if someone has trespassed on someone else's land, it's a civil and not a criminal offence. You could take your neighbours to court and get an injunction ordering them not to trespass in future.

"Or," he went on, "you could eject them yourself, and if you do that you're allowed to use reasonable force."

After the law had gone, I thought about that for a bit. Not for long, because I could feel the anger surging up inside me. Soon I was exploding and I flew down to the woods. The neighbours had gone back to their gardens so I stood there calling for them – "Come out, you thieving ————s!" It was like *Bonanza*.

When they came back, one of them stopped with his nose sticking over the boundary line, so I tapped it for him. I was fighting mad. I pointed to the perimeter.

"You want the land?" I shouted. "You come and get it. You step over that line and I'll break your bleeding nose!"

The language was really flowing now. Behind me Mr Carroll, an Irishman who was then our gardener, came up and tried to pacify me: "Come away now, Mr Willis."

I was having none of it. I was ready to take on the lot of them. Then Cilla arrived with our Robert in his pram. On the other side of the line, more neighbours were coming out, including some who hadn't been trying to grab our land. Some of them took our side, and started accusing the others of thieving. So then a new round of arguments broke out, with neighbour shouting at neighbour. Very un-English it was; chaos on a Sunday afternoon in the heart of Buckinghamshire.

That phase of the battle ended with more lip from me and shouts of: "You want a fence? I'll show you a flaming fence!" (or words to that effect). I stormed back to the house with Cilla, the pram, the gardener and the dogs and started planning the fence I was going to build. If I'd had the materials there and then, it would have been higher than the Berlin Wall, and fitted out with searchlights and machine-gun posts.

When I'd calmed down slightly, I decided to run an eight-foot chain- mail fence all round the perimeter. Then I found you had to apply to the council for anything higher than six feet, so I settled on that. And that is what we've now got – except in one place where a 'good' neighbour came round and said it would spoil his view. He had a good enough wooden fence at the back of his garden, so I agreed to stop our fence when it reached his property and re-start it on the other side. The 'baddies' were fenced off, but this feller kept his view.

It didn't end there, but I'll let Cilla tell you what happened.'

****

It didn't end there because some of the neighbours were stung by the way Bobby had put them in their place. We had a deputation come to the door.

'We're from the local Residents' Association,' they said.

'I'm a resident too,' said Bobby 'Doesn't that include me?'

That was nearly the end of that particular conversation. But we did talk to them, and we didn't get anywhere much because they were a real pain and very patronizing to us 'pop stars'. So that didn't clear the air either, and the next thing I heard they'd given their side of the story to the papers. I had to go away to do some filming, and I caught the next episode over the phone.

Bobby and I were in Geilo, in Norway, filming on a mountaintop with Ringo Starr and Basil Brush. I got back to the hotel and rang home to see if everything was all right. I spoke to Pat, my girlfriend, who was staying at the house.

'Oh,' she said, 'you're on the front of the *Sunday Express*'

'What are you talking about?' I said.

'It's a lovely picture,' she said.

'Yes,' I said, 'but what am I doing in the paper? What's going on?'

'Well,' she said, 'it's says something like "Bobby Willis says, if you want my blank blank land, you'll have to blank well come and get it. You're all a shower of blank thieves." '

Then she read out some of the article, which was full of these 'blanks'. 'Mr Willis said: "Blank blank blank blank." ' That kind of thing.

I said to her: 'Pat, why do you keep saying "Blank"?'

'Well, that's what it's got in the article,' she replied. 'It's full of dashes going "blank blank" across the page.'

Still I didn't get it. 'What are they for?' I wanted to know.

'I think they're all swearwords!' she said. According to the story in the newspaper, Bobby had let rip with all sorts of insults about "You blank middle-class Southerners, you think you own everything, you robbing blank blank so-and-sos."

Now it was really out of hand. Instead of a dispute between a few neighbours, it had become a war, fought out on the frontiers of class, background, North versus South, everything bar the kitchen sink.

Every so often anyone in the public eye is likely to find themselves getting a mauling in the press. When this happens to me, the only person I am worried about is my Mum. She is a God-fearing lady and I thought she might have been upset about all the 'blanks' which had seemed to come more from our side – or Bobby. So I rang her up, and she was one hundred per cent behind us.

'Yes,' she said. 'Who do they think they are, those Southerners!' Bobby was not only not to blame with my mother, he was on his way to becoming a folk hero. Soon after that, we were filming on Liverpool's ground and Bill Shankly, their wonderful old manager, called Bobby over.

In his gritty voice, Shanks said: 'You did well, son. If the President of the United States can punch a critic on the nose for criticizing his daughter, you're entitled to call the Southern bastards "Southern bastards".'

The incident with the American President was a few years before Bill Shankly came out in support of us, but I gather it's true that Whoever-it-was, while he was still President, walked up and clocked a critic for being unkind in a report about his daughter, who was going round in a terrible cabaret act. 'That's for my daughter,' he said, after he'd belted the reporter. 'I'm a father first, before I'm the president.'

It was amazing to me how our little argument in Buckinghamshire had boiled up into a national affair. It wasn't until our neighbours had started putting us down with snide remarks about Northerners, and suggestions like 'Why don't you go back where you came from?' that I realized what strong feelings there were down in these so-called refined Southern parts.

Letters came flooding in. On the 'hate' side there were messages like 'We don't want your kind here.' On the 'for us' side people wrote in to say well done and 'If you want any help we'll come down and kick them for you.' It split the country. We even had a letter from some Pakistanis in Birmingham.

They said: 'We'll move into their gardens and squat there. That'll make the price of their properties go down.'

We said nothing publicly. We didn't try to reply through the newspaper or anything, because that would not have helped. It even seems quite funny now that people should get so het up about where their neighbours were born, but the whole business had reached a silly stage as far as we were concerned. The awkward ones among our neighbours had even got them-selves a solicitor. To settle it once and for all, we asked Lord Goodman to act for us and he sent them a letter explaining that they would be sued if they went on bothering us or trespassed on our property.

This finally silenced them, and with time the problem seems to have gone away. But it still seems to me they had a terrible cheek trying to pinch our land. Apparently, if we'd done nothing about it for twelve years, they would have been able to claim squatters' rights over all the ground they had fenced in.

When we put up our own fence, part of it ran next to the land of our famous neighbour and friend, Roger Moore. He had a stream in his garden which started from a spring and then flowed into our property. While all this business was going on, he jokingly said to us:

'I'm going to block up that stream! You're not having my water.'

Today, after fifteen peaceful years in our house in Denham, that whole episode seems very distant, like an extraordinary dream. As for the North v South conflict, Bobby and I are getting on to being adopted Southerners ourselves, and our children certainly are. Our Robert even supports Watford!

Admittedly, I've never lost my Livepool accent, and I never want to. But the boys are bilingual. Our Jack, who's four, talks to visitors in Southern English, but for me he goes into thick Scouse. At the back of his mind, I can see him thinking: 'Well, if I don't talk like that, she won't understand me.'

I almost wish I'd been born Spanish or Italian, because by now our boys would be bilingual in another language plus English – instead of just being able to speak Scouse and Normal.

✳✳✳✳

In the end, like it or not, we would have had to put up a proper fence be-cause of our dogs. Ada and Sophie, our two Briards, were starting to get into other people's gardens, and we were afraid that they might bite somebody.

In her time Ada probably bit about thirty people, not seriously or because she was a vicious animal but because it was in her nature to de-fend her home territory. On the other hand, she was marvellous with kids. But when we first moved to the house, people were forever wandering in off the road. On Sunday afternoons we'd get troops of cars coming down our drive like we were part of a sightseeing tour. 'Oh, sorry,' they'd say if we challenged them. 'I thought it was a road.'

One day the vicar came round and Ada bit him in the private parts –

With the family at our villa in the south of Spain.

only bruising him, fortunately, but we had to get him a new pair of trousers.

She bit the paper boy and he stopped coming. Then she bit the postman and now he leaves all the letters at the cottage. One day she had a builder pinned up against a wall when he tried to walk out of the house carrying a plank. Ada would let strangers take things into the house, but she didn't like them taking anything out again.

She was a fine intelligent animal – she couldn't be daft if she won Best of Rare Breeds at Cruft's – but people sometimes forget that certain dogs are bred to look after their owners' property. And with a house like ours we have to be careful. We had our first burglary before we'd even moved into the place; they pinched all our wedding presents. Now we are better organized. We have an electric gate so that anyone wanting to come to the house by the normal route has to buzz us on the intercom so we can open the gate and let them in.

We have a Doberman as well, but he spends most of his time patrolling the perimeter and looking out for the deer which live in the woods round here. He's called Panzer – and he looks like one! He is an amazing dog, because although he can seem terrifying to outsiders, he adores the kids and is a marvellous family pet.

My favourite story about our dogs has to do with Ada after she had won the award at Cruft's. I was so proud of her, I wanted to have her on the live Saturday evening show.

Now Ada was a very clever dog. At the drop of a hat she could do all the party tricks – 'Give us your paw,' 'Roll over,' all that stuff. Well, when it was her turn, and after I had introduced her and told the audience what she'd done that afternoon just up the road at Olympia, she made her entrance. She looked ever so pretty, with her beautiful coat and her winner's rosette.

I told the audience that I would get Ada to do a few of her tricks, beginning with 'Sit'. So I gave her the command and she just lay down at my feet and refused to get up! 'Come on Ada,' I said. 'It's "Sit!" Not "Lie down".' No good. I tried her with 'Give us your paw'; she didn't move. I tried again and noticed her eyes were shut and her body was heaving up and down with deep regular breaths.

Now the audience was beginning to snicker and titter. 'Come on, girl,' I said to Ada, picking up one of her front paws. 'You can do it.'

The paw was all floppy when I held it. The rest of Ada made no effort to get up or even look at me. Then I heard this deep 'whuffling' noise: the unmistakeable sound of a dog snoring. Under the heat of the studio lights, added to the long hours she'd spent in the ring at Olympia, Ada had finally given in to exhaustion. There was no stirring her. My efforts to turn a sleeping dog into a performing dog were getting more and more like a bad music hall act. I gave up.

We still had an item to fill, so at the next link-in I said to the camera: 'If there's anybody watching at home, and you live near the studio and you've got a dog that's as clever as mine, bring them along and we'll interview you and your dog outside.'

Millions of dogs came. We even had some celebrity dogs. They completely blocked Shepherds Bush Green and no other traffic could get through. The fire engines had to be called out to clear a way. We had every dog under the sun including a dog on heat that was being assaulted by a couple of older dogs, while the owners had a shouting match – 'Why don't you keep that one locked up?' 'I shouldn't have to. Why don't you keep yours under control?' There was fighting, barking, yelping, pulling at the leads, marking all the lampposts for miles around. The dogs were in their element. And not just the dogs.

The cameras picked up a feller who'd brought his stuffed lion along. Then in the queue, waiting to be interviewed, I saw another feller with a stuffed parrot on his shoulder. I looked down at his feet but couldn't see a dog.

I said to him: 'Now, look. Come on. It's supposed to be dogs. Why have you got a stuffed parrot on your shoulder? What can that do?'

He said: 'It's got a bloody sight more life in it than your dog!'

FAMILY
AND FRIENDS

*'When Robert went into hospital to have his tonsils
and adenoids out, I was working at the Victoria
Palace till eleven o 'clock at night. I must have been
the first Women's Libber who had the freedom but
didn't want it. It should have been me – the mother –
sleeping on the camp bed in the hospital next to
Robert, instead of which Bobby had to do it.'*

I might add, it's a good thing Bobby did do it.
He is so controlled, he is marvellous at comfort-
ing people and making them feel there's nothing really wrong with them. Whereas, let's admit
it, I do get a bit emotional at times, and can't
help letting my own feelings take over.

When I took our Ben to school on his first
day, I started the whole class crying. My trouble
was, I couldn't leave him. I kept going back. 'Are
you alright?' I was asking him. 'Yes,' he said. 'Are
you sure?' I insisted. 'Yes,' he said. I got to the
door and then went back. 'You're not to worry,'

I told him. 'It's only two hours, and then we'll be back for you.' 'Yes, I know,' he said.

Bobby was there as well, and he said: 'Come on, let's just leave him, let's go.'

I looked at Bobby, then back at Ben – and burst into tears. That started the whole class off. Everybody except the teacher and Bobby was howling and whimpering all over the place. In the end they threw me out – and when Jack started at the same school six years later, they banned me from taking him on the first day.

So you can see, it's a good thing our Robert had Bobby with him in the hospital. Poor Robert, he was six at the time, and it was only after we started seeing a specialist that we found he was suffering from acute sinusitis. This meant he'd probably been going around for ages – or ever since he developed the condition – with a permanent headache. I know you can get used to most things, but imagine walking around with a headache all the time, to the point where you accept that it's normal and probably think that everybody else must have one. He never complained; as a baby he was always marvellous and gave no trouble, but with the sinusitis he was almost too perfect for his own good.

Having Robert changed my life. He changed my life so completely, I hardly know where to begin describing all that happened. Because of Robert, we left London and moved out to our house in Buckinghamshire. I carried on working because I had no wish to retire, which anyway wouldn't have made sense. And because of this, we found ourselves entering a new world – the world of nannies.

Remember, I could get no immediate help from friends or relatives. Where we lived, there were no aunties or grandmothers living round the corner who could pop in for me. My girlfriends, like Cathy McGowan and Pat Davies, were all up in London – in fact I was the first pop mum of that generation. So although, in Liverpool, a nanny is your grandmother, I had to get used to the fact that I needed the other sort of nanny – the posh sort. Maybe she'd even wear a uniform!

To begin with, we had Nurse Bobbie. We knew her already, because we inherited her from George and Judy Martin, whose kids she had looked after. Nurse Bobbie was wonderful, one of the old school; she looked after babies for the first six months of their life, and she was all for me going off for a month and taking a rest, because that's what mothers from well-to-do families always did in the old days. Me, I didn't want to go anywhere, I couldn't bear the thought of letting Robert out of my sight for a minute longer than I had to. But there was no friction: we all got along together very well, and without Nurse Bobbie I don't know how I'd have got through those first six months.

It was Nurse Bobbie who encouraged me to get away from London and move into our house before it was really ready for us. That didn't matter, she said, the baby should have the fresh air. So down we came to Denham.

Anyone who has had her first baby will know that it can be quite a frightening experience for the first few months. Whether or not you have the means to afford a live-in nanny – and in any case, because of work, I had no choice – it's your responsibility to make sure the baby is properly cared for. What terrified me most of all was when Nurse Bobbie had a day off, and I was left to make all the decisions but had no-one local to ring up if I had a worry.

In fact, I must have felt more isolated than I actually was. When Robert got a spot on his face, I could have phoned the local doctor, but I didn't. I rang up our paediatrician, Dr Sam Tucker, who had examined Robert at birth in the Avenue Clinic, St John's Wood.

'Please come round,' I said, 'Robert's got this spot on his face.'

He was marvellous about it. He came and looked at Robert, who did have a spot on his face but he said it was nothing to worry about. However, he put my mind at rest, and that was probably the most valuable part of his visit – for us all!

Soon Nurse Bobbie's time was up, because she only ever stayed for the first three to six months while the mother got settled in with her new baby. To take her place, we found a local girl, Jenny. Or, to be more accurate, she found us.

It must have been in the papers somewhere that Nurse Bobbie was leaving and that we hadn't found a successor, because one day Jenny walked over the golf course from where she lived, knocked on the door and said to Nurse Bobbie:

'I hear you're leaving. I'd like to take over the job when you go.'

When I heard about this, I was horrified. I thought: 'You can't give a job to someone who just comes round and knocks on your front door.'

But Nurse Bobbie was much more relaxed about it, and she supported Jenny. She said:

'I have a feeling about this girl. She's a good girl. I've talked to her, and I've seen her with Robert, and I think she'd be ideal. Besides, she lives just over the golf course, her mother's there, and on her days off she's got friends in the community, and that could be a great help to you.'

So Jenny came, and Nurse Bobbie was right. She was very good with Robert and it was a marvellous time. Jenny wasn't trained for the job, but that didn't seem to matter. After a while we found that what she really wanted to do was to be an air hostess. With the way I love flying, I thought she was totally mad! Anyway, we gave her some good references and she went off to train with one of the airlines and eventually she did qualify as an air hostess.

Our next nanny, Penny, has been with us ever since, which is fourteen years so far. She came to us through a more orthodox channel, answering an advertisement in one of the specialist magazines. She was very young and her sister came with her to the interview, which was conducted by a rather nervous me because I wasn't that old myself and didn't really know what to ask. Anyway, Bobby and I both liked her, she had all the right qualifications, and so we offered her the job. She came to live with us, and on her first evening she passed another very important test.

My cooking has never been one of my strongest assets. I buy all the cookery books but never do anything with them. I can manage a few starters, and roast a piece of meat, but when it comes to desserts and baking things, I'm lost. You can ask Bobby, who trained as a baker and confectioner, whether I'm hopeless or not. Once, with his help, I made a sensational bread pudding for Robert and he woofed the lot, but my triumphs in the kitchen are few and far between. Our Ben likes my Yorkshire puddings, but I haven't had the heart to tell him that I buy them from the deep-freeze place. One day, unfortunately, he will have to face the fact that his Mum is the Queen of Frozen Pastry.

While Nurse Bobbie was with us, she never did any cooking and it was always down to us to provide all the meals. It wasn't that she couldn't cook, she very sensibly didn't see it as part of her job to cook meals – and she no doubt also saw that this was a duty she could very easily have got lumbered with if she'd shown much willing.

In London, when we were in the flat, it was easy. If we needed a meal, we'd ring up these posh Mayfair caterers who'd come round and lay down all this marvellous food in front of us. That was wonderful. But where in Denham do you ring up a posh caterer?

Well, I had to accept that Denham was more heavily into self-catering than I was used to, and so the struggle began to feed the starving Willises and their nanny. On Penny's first night, I planned to cook a shepherd's pie. It came out really vile, I don't know why, it just did. It was so horrible, I couldn't eat mine. But Penny ate all hers, and I was struck with this profound thought: if she can eat my cooking, she can't be half bad.

Penny has been with us from that day. She has made a very important contribution to the way we operate as a show-business family, keeping strange hours and going off to foreign parts on working trips that we usually tackle at breakneck speed, looking after the boys if they are with us, or taking charge at home if we have to be away without them. She has been round the world with us three times, and is very much part of the family.

All that was still in the future when, soon after Penny joined us I found out – oh, deep joy and what bliss! – that she was also a very good cook. I mean, she actually enjoyed making cakes! I'm not particularly proud of the fact that I have never made a gingerbread man for one of my kids, simply because I can't, but at least with Penny there I know they are getting their fair share, and now she even lets our Jack make his own.

✳✳✳✳

Someone else who has helped us a tremendous lot over the years is my friend Pat Davies. She and I go back all the way to Liverpool. We went out to the clubs together, and we both went through a phase of wanting to be a hairdresser.

That meant finding someone to practise on, but neither of our Mums would let us near their hair. The only woman we ever met who didn't mind us doing the practical work on her was Ringo's mother, Elsie Starkey. On Wednesday nights we went round to her house and she was the soul of patience. She let us bleach her hair and do terrible things to it, but she never once complained. She also gave us our tea – either boiled ham or spam and home-made chips. Mrs Starkey was a fantastic lady and still is. The other day I was sorry I had to miss going to Ringo's forty-fifth birthday party, because his Mum was coming down from Liverpool for it. Just think, when I was eighteen I went to his twenty-first.

To go back to my friend Pat, we relied on her a lot when the boys were small. She had her own keys to the house and she used to come down whenever she wanted. Especially at weekends, when we were away and Penny had the weekend off, we were much happier if Pat was around to keep an eye on things and look after the boys. You can get people from an agency, but it's never as reassuring as having someone you've known all your life.

When I wasn't there, Pat didn't mess around, she was the complete substitute mother. One day when she was at the house, Bobby was boiling a ham. He told Pat it would be ready at such-and-such a time, and then we both went out.

The time came to serve up the joint, and Pat was surprised to find that the boys didn't like it.

'Come on,' she told them, 'you eat that up. Your Dad's cooked that specially for you.'

Ben led the protests, and none of them liked the bacon joint, but Pat was a stickler for making sure kids did what they were told, and in the end they emptied their plates. When Bobby got back, Ben had already been sick and looked as miserable as sin. So Bobby looked at the ham and found it was only half-cooked. Whether Pat had misunderstood Bobby over the cooking time, I don't know, but she certainly took it off the heat when it was barely half-done, and then made the boys eat every scrap she gave them!

Robert, of course, has known Pat a good deal longer than either Ben or Jack. He's fifteen now, and says his ideal woman is a brunette. If you ask him why, he says it's because he can't stand being bossed about by blondes (Pat is a blonde) or redheads (me!). But Pat and I don't mind. We're waiting to see what happens when he runs out of colours.

Pat has been a wonderful friend to us all, and she has a heart of gold. I miss her now, because eighteen months ago she got married and – worse still-went off to live in the United States. We could have seen it coming, but we ignored the clues. When we made the pilot show for *Surprise Surprise,* we had a Jamaican lady who predicted the future by laying a piece of tissue over her subject's face and collecting an 'aura' from which she could tell their fortune. She told Biggins he would be going to Australia – which he did, although at the time he had no plans to go – and she told Pat that she would go to America and stay there. She did. She married an American producer and now lives in New York. How's that for a 100 per cent prediction?

****

By the way, I never told you about our wedding, did I? It's quite a saga really, but I'll just give you the highlights. It all began one Tuesday night at a dinner when Peter Brown, Brian Epstein's assistant, said to me and Bobby:

'Why don't you two get married?'

It was something that we'd have got round to one day, but we were in no hurry. So Bobby said to him:

'We don't really want the hassle. But if you arrange it, we'll do it.'

So he did. He said: 'Right, it's your birthday on Saturday. We'll have it then.'

Next day we had a production meeting to plan my next show. The phone rang and Bobby answered it. On the other end was Peter saying: 'I'm downstairs. Come on, we're going to Marylebone Registrar's Office.'

Bobby turned to me. 'Peter's downstairs. What d'you reckon?'

'OK,' I said, 'you might as well go.'

That was my proposal of marriage! So, without a word to anyone else,

Bobby went off to see the registrar and get the banns announced. Almost as soon as the notice went up, our secrecy was blown. Some clever so-and-so spotted that Priscilla Maria Veronica White was down to marry Robert Willis, and it was plastered all over the newspapers.

Well, my mother, when she heard! The thing was, Bobby and I didn't want any fuss, we just wanted to get married quietly. On Friday my mother was on the phone, very upset. 'My only daughter, doing this to me without so much as a word.. You're not in any kind of trouble, are you?'

'No,' I said. 'We just wanted to do it quietly.'

Well, they all came down from Liverpool. They didn't like the idea of a registrar's office, and the only way I could pacify them was to agree to have a white wedding later in Liverpool, when we had time.

At the ceremony, everyone seemed nervous except me. Some people were shaking all over, and I even had a word with the registrar because he looked as if he was going to forget his lines!

'Come on,' I said, 'let's have a dress rehearsal.'

So then he calmed down and we got on with it. A few weeks later we went up to Liverpool for the special service and blessing. My mother wanted to book the Catholic Cathedral but the Monsignor refused because we'd got married already. So we went to my mother's local church, St Mary's. It was a big posh do with hundreds of guests, a lot of them up from London. The reception was at the Adelphi.

Well, the Adelphi is *the* poshest place in Liverpool. When I was at school, I wouldn't have dared go up two steps at the front of the place. It was everyone's ambition to win the pools and stay the night at the Adelphi. Now I was having a wedding reception there.

Half of our family were terrified of going in there, but we got them all in, had a few drinks, then:

'Order! Order!'

This flunky put a microphone on the table and everybody had to behave themselves. Then Bobby's brother Kenny started reading out the telegrams, but he was nervous as well and Bobby had to take over from him. As soon as he'd finished, in front of all these smart people from London, my Uncle Jimmy got up, grabbed the microphone and started singing!

At an ordinary wedding in Liverpool, that is what would have happened anyway. Everyone who wanted to would have done a turn. But in the Adelphi! I couldn't believe it. I looked round nervously at all the up-market folk we had with us that day – and they were loving it!

✳✳✳✳

Robert was not only the perfect baby who never complained, he also survived my best efforts to finish him off quick. When he was six months old, I was working in pantomime at the London Palladium and it was coming up to Christmas. As luck would have it, Christmas Day fell at the weekend and I had two whole days off. Nurse Bobbie went to spend Christmas in Wales, and Bobby and I spent the holiday on our own – not forgetting Robert.

Usually we had guests in the house. My mother would come down from Liverpool, sometimes with Auntie Nellie, and Pat would be with us because she had no immediate family. But that year the pantomime made it very difficult to have anyone to stay because Bobby and I would have been getting up and leaving them all the time – except for the two days I had off.

It was our first Christmas at the house, and the memory of it is something we treasure. Snow fell on Christmas Day, and in the rose garden one red rose was in bloom. As usual, Robert was no trouble at all. I put him in his big pram and wheeled him round the garden, and then I left him outside for a while in the lovely crisp air – Nurse Bobbie said that fresh air, in all weathers, was good for babies – and went into the house. Later in the morning I went out to check how he was, and he was asleep. Bobby and I got on with preparing our Christmas dinner, and when I went out to look at the baby, he slept on.

I phoned my mother and told her how perfect everything was on this beautiful Christmas morning. I told her about the snow and the red rose which had come out.

'It's really wonderful, Mum,' I went on, 'and the baby is marvellous. I can't believe how well behaved our Robert is, all by himself in the garden. He must have been out there for three hours . . .'

My mother said: 'Get-that-baby-in-immediately.'

The tone of her voice was enough. I never said another word, just put the phone down and ran outside, Bobby following because he'd seen my expression change. I picked Robert out of his pram and he was still asleep.

'Is he alright?' Bobby was asking, looking over my shoulder.

'Yes,' I said guiltily, 'of course he is,' and jiggled Robert about furiously to wake him. In a few moments, thank God, he opened his eyes and looked around, but without much interest. Poor thing, although he was awake, he felt as sleepy as anything. What I hadn't realized was that it may be good for babies to leave them outdoors in winter – but not for three hours when the temperature is below freezing! The cold just makes them sleepier and sleepier, while their body temperature sinks and sinks. Need I go on, except to say that, but for my Mum, he could be out there yet!

Robert was born in July 1970, and Ben arrived in April 1974. Unlike

Robert's birth which was trouble-free, Ben was born in a manner which, if I'd had him first, would have left me saying: 'Enough. One baby is all I need.'

Ben was already a fortnight overdue when I went to have yet another check-up with my consultant, Professor Geoffrey Chamberlain, in his Harley Street surgery.

'Well,' he said, 'if nothing happens soon, we're going to have to bring your baby on.'

'That suits me fine,' I said, because by that time all the waiting was getting on my nerves – as it does with most women who have to suffer all that extra stress at a time when they least of all need it. I just wanted the birth to be over and done with.

'How would it be,' I went on, 'if you induced me on May the First. 'Cos I'd really love a May Day baby.'

Bobby was there, and he suddenly looked very thoughtful. Eventually he said: 'I don't think we can have May the First, because Professor Chamberlain won't be at the hospital that day. That's his day for being here in Harley Street.

'Also,' Bobby went on, 'that's the day Liverpool are playing Juventus in the European Cup.'

It was my baby, but I had no choice about when it could be born. I just sat there while these two men – one of them my husband, the other my consultant – discussed their various movements during that week! Luckily, they were able to agree on a date which suited both of them – April 30th – and that was the day it actually happened.

Three days before I was due to go in, I was sitting at home watching television when I felt this tremendous lurch in my stomach. As I looked down, the great lump in my tummy that was Ben rolled right over to one side. Then he seemed to tumble downwards, before rolling across to the other side.

Bobby jumped up off the couch. 'What's that? What's that?'

I couldn't explain what had happened. It was really odd. I didn't feel any pain, but if Ben was trying to get someone to let him out, he couldn't have sent a better message! But then he settled down again, and we had no more alarms before it was time for me to go into hospital and we set off in the car, with Bobby, incidentally, singing 'Amy, Amy . . . pure as the driven snow' because at that stage he was convinced I was going to have a girl.

In the hospital a young feller, who looked about fourteen, examined me. He said: 'Your baby has turned completely round. Instead of his head being in the downward position, ready to be born, he has turned round so that now he's lying feet down.'

So now we knew what Ben had been up to that evening. 'I'm fed up with lying like this,' he must have thought to himself. 'I'm going to have a change.' And that was how he was born – feet first, a breech birth. He's still called 'Ben the Breech' in the family, and he's been doing things back to front ever since!

Fortunately, I still had the memory of Robert's birth which had been nice and easy, so I wasn't put off the whole baby business for ever, and in 1980 I had a third boy, our Jack.

It's one thing to give birth, but quite another to keep your kids alive long enough so they're able to look after themselves. All boys seem to have this ability to pick fights with objects that are heavier and thicker than they are, and my three have certainly paid their dues. Probably the worst was Ben, who went through a terrible phase of being accident-prone.

If he fell over, he never put his hands out to break his fall, he always went completely flat – like Bugs Bunny or Sylvester the Cat – and got bashed all over. One day, just before we were going off to Spain on holiday, Ben fell out of the gardener's wheelbarrow onto the concrete floor of the garage. He looked as if he'd been in a car crash. His nose was bruised and bleeding and he had two black eyes! Still, he wasn't unfit to travel and so we went to Spain.

Nearly everyone we met during our holiday was sympathetic towards us when they saw poor Ben, but I will always remember one loud-mouthed woman who wasn't. We were in a restaurant and she came up and said to Ben:

'Ooh! And what has your Mummy been doing to you?'

It really upset me, getting this from a complete stranger who didn't know anything about our family. I became really self-conscious about Ben and didn't want anybody else to see him till he was better and his bruising had gone down.

It didn't worry Ben, who was in no hurry to get better. Because he was so accident-prone, he fell over at least a couple more times on the parts of him that were black and blue already, and finished up with bumps on his bumps on his bumps!

That incident reminds me of another difficult time a few years before, when I was voted Celebrity Mum of the Year. Robert was only six weeks old, and perhaps the novelty of me being a mum had won me a few extra votes but I was really quite pleased to have come top of the poll (beating the Queen who came third).

I went along to the reception wearing a pair of hotpants and looking no more like a mum than our Robert himself. Anyway, the press and radio all wanted to know how my baby was, and I told them I'd had to leave the house so early that morning I hadn't seen him. This wasn't in fact true because I had seen him while he was still asleep but then I'd had to dash off to London, leaving him in the hands of Nurse Bobbie.

There was a little fracas over that, but the important thing is to believe in yourself, which I have always managed to do. Everyone in my position has to remember that these things can also affect their family. Back home in Liverpool we have got my mother and brothers to think of, and Bobby's family as well, and the last thing we want is people coming up to them and making sni- dey comments. They aren't in show business themselves, and they don't necessarily know what's been going on in the first place, so they won't know what to think or say, and the effect of that can be very upsetting. So, over the years, I've tried to 'train' my family, especially my mother, in the ways of the press and how to respond to them. I always let her know when something important is going to happen, so she is forewarned if the press contact her. Recently, when I went into hospital to have a hysterectomy, I rang up and told her as soon as I knew.

'Oh,' she said, 'you're not having one of them hysterical operations are you?'

Well, at least I'd told her!

Although I've said that my family aren't in show business, by a funny process they do become mini-celebrities in their own right. My mother is the best example, and it's been going on a long time now. If an organization couldn't get me for a charity opening or a fete up in Liverpool, they'd ask my mother. After a while, they stopped asking me, and that's when I found it was because they'd *rather* have me Mum. She's a market woman, she's still got her own stall, and she's very outgoing and funny, much funnier than me. Also, she would have more time to spend at these functions, so she became favourite over me.

One Sunday, not long after I'd had two No 1 hits, I was walking along Scotland Road and someone called out: 'Ey, Cilla, you think you can sing. You're rubbish. Your Mum's much better than you.'

Since then, she's gone from strength to strength!

****

Thinking of Liverpool, it's strange what an effect it had on our boys when we took them up there. Although Bobby and I have always loved living in our big house surrounded by seventeen acres of grounds, it can have its drawbacks with children. Our boys can't just nip next door to play whenever they want; they have to have it organized for them, and be taken everywhere by car.

When we took Robert and Ben up to Liverpool, where I was in

pantomime at the Empire, they were actually amazed that all the people there lived side by side in streets full of terraced houses. We were in Kenny's house – he's one of Bobby's brothers – and the boys couldn't believe it. They kept running up and down the stairs like it was some kind of big treehouse, and Robert actually said to me:

'Why can't we live in a house like this?'

I didn't know what to say. It really touched my heart, and brought home to me that what really counts is not the size of your house or garden, or whether you've got a swimming pool, but the area you live in and the people you are surrounded by.

Kenny, on the other hand, who actually lived there, took a different view. He was glad to get out of that little house as soon as he could and move to a bigger one in Moreton. Maybe that's the story of Liverpool – a place that people leave if they get the chance, but then their kids see it and think it's such a great place, they want to move back there!

Even my mother, who still works in Liverpool, was glad to move away from Scotland Road. Not that she could have stayed there, because all our part has been flattened. At one stage the council were threatening to renovate our flat over the barber's shop, which terrified me Mum because she wanted to be rehoused and have a proper council house with its own bathroom and front door. Anyway, as soon as I had made a bit of money, I bought me Mum and Dad a brand-new detached home up in Woolton. It had a bathroom, central heating, french windows, its own front door and a lovely front garden. It was a beautiful house and me Dad was thrilled with it. Me Mum said:

'It's very nice, but couldn't you have got us a house with a bus stop outside?'

She went on complaining about not being near a bus stop for some time, and in the end I asked her if she wanted to move back down.

'Oh, no,' she said. 'No, no.'

✳✳✳✳

Robert and Ben had their final proof that Liverpool is a magical place when Bobby took them and Penny to see *Superman*. It was in one of those new 1, 2, 3 cinemas, very modern-looking with a banked stage under the screen.

They all enjoyed the trailer, the short, then the main film, with Christopher Reeves as Superman. When it came to an end, and as the credits were running up the screen, a young kid jumped on the stage. He had his mac buttoned round his neck so that it flowed out behind him, and he was per-' fectly silhouetted on the screen behind him. Then he made his run, a series of

Super-leaps, with his arms pointing out in front of him, all the way across the stage. Penny and Bobby were in stitches at this lad, but our boys couldn't work it out.

'What's he doing?' they asked.

'I don't know,' said Bobby, 'but you're in Liverpool now.'

✳✳✳✳

When we're at home, and I'm not working, we tend to keep to ourselves and don't do a lot of entertaining. All our friends know that they are more than welcome to drop in whenever they like and we will be delighted to see them. They also know that they are taking a chance on the cooking, but that's the way we are. If people arrive without warning, I think to myself: 'Oh, good. I don't have to worry about the food,' cos if it's no good, they've only got themselves to blame.

I will sit and chat to people for hours, but if I have to keep getting up and going outside to check on the meal I get quite agitated and put out. In fact, I'd much rather appear live in front of twenty million viewers than have four people to dinner.

If there's one friend who's taken all this in his stride, it's Frankie Howerd. He understands very well that the best way to visit us is to ring up and invite himself, which is great. He's almost one of the family. In his time he's taken me Mum down to Midnight Mass on Christmas Eve – and been propositioned by my Auntie Nellie. She wagged her eyelashes at him one evening and said:

'I'm a widow, you know.'

Frankie was captivated, and now he loves her deeply, but mostly at a distance of at least two hundred miles. He has probably found out that Auntie Nellie has done this to a lot of other eligible fellers. Sometimes she overdoes it and we all shout at her: 'Of course you're a widow, Auntie Nellie. Only widows go on like that!'

Frankie is also a great favourite with our kids, and he thinks the world of them. A few years ago he arrived one evening just as Robert and Ben were getting ready for bed. They wanted Frankie to go and see them, so he went upstairs. He sat down on the bed next to Ben and gave him one of his big smiles – and Ben burst into tears. Frankie was quite upset.

'Oh,' he said. 'No. No, look. No, look it's only me, come to say goodnight. Come on, cheer up.'

But Ben just carried on sobbing his heart out.

'Oh, dear,' said Frankie, 'I didn't want you to get all excited. I mean. . .

When we were four. Bobby and me with Robert (right) and Ben during my 1978 season at the Princess Theatre. Torquay.

Then we were five. Soon after the birth of our Jack in 1980.

A picture from the old days – with my friend Pat in the Cavern Club, Liverpool.

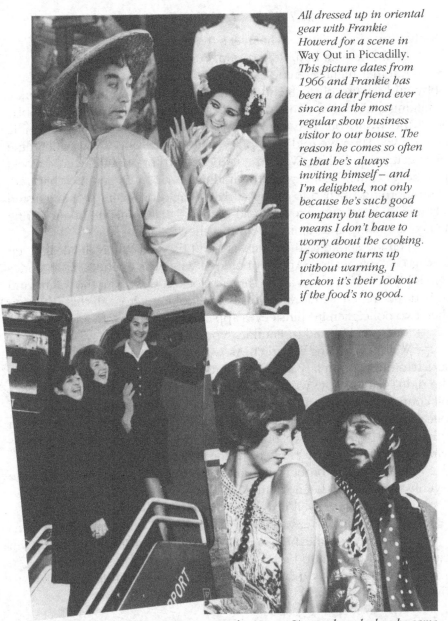

All dressed up in oriental gear with Frankie Howerd for a scene in Way Out in Piccadilly. This picture dates from 1966 and Frankie has been a dear friend ever since and the most regular show business visitor to our house. The reason he comes so often is that he's always inviting himself – and I'm delighted, not only because he's such good company but because it means I don't have to worry about the cooking. If someone turns up without warning, I reckon it's their lookout if the food's no good.

Two shots of me with Ringo Starr – at Speke Airport, Liverpool, and when he came on my TV show as a special guest. He has been a very good friend over the years, and his Mum, Elsie Starkey, was the only mum who'd let me and my friend Pat practise on her hair when we thought we were going to be hairdressers. We bleached it, and did terrible things to it, but she never once complained – a wonderful lady.

When the airport picture was taken, I was in The Beatles' show at the Finsbury Park Empire, and we would have had to spend Christmas in London except that, as a surprise present, Brian Epstein hired a plane and offered to fly the whole cast up to Liverpool. The only one who didn't want to go was Rolf Harris!

it's only your Uncle Frank. Whatever's the matter?'

From the next bed, Robert said: 'You're sitting on his foot.'

Another night, Frankie came down to see us with his sister Betty. Bobby and I were off to Spain at ten o'clock the next day, but Frankie got talking and told us some of his amazing stories. Then he and Bobby sorted the world out between them, as they usually do when Frankie come down. Then we told each other a few more stories, by which time it was getting quite late. We had a taxi ordered for about eleven o'clock, but it never came. Now it was after midnight and I was getting a bit tired. In the morning we had to be up early to pack for Spain, so I suggested to Frankie – because we're such old friends – that someone ought to ring the taxi company and remind them that they're late.

Frankie spoke to them himself, and they said their driver had left ages ago. So, we waited. Another bottle of wine was opened, more stories were told, and soon it was about three o'clock. It was a very hot night, and we had the french windows open. I was looking across in that direction when two policemen in shirtsleeves appeared, together with another feller.

'Oh, good,' I said to Frankie, 'your taxi's arrived.'

Well, it had, and it hadn't. As we found out from the policemen, there had been a burglary at the bottom of the road, and the taxi driver – who didn't really know where we were except that our house was near a golf course – had been found on one of the fairways, behaving, or so the police thought, in a suspicious manner. They pounced on him, and then he had a lot of trouble explaining that he was a taxi driver and he was trying to pick up Frankie Howerd from our address.

So the police brought him along to the house and we were able to verify that we had been waiting for him.

'Good,' I said, 'well now you can take Mr Howerd home.'

'It's not quite as easy as that, madam,' said one of the policemen.

'What do you mean?' I said. 'It's late, it's four in the morning, I'm dead tired and I've got to be up early to pack and go to Spain.'

'The problem is, madam, that we can't allow this gentleman to drive away.'

'Why ever not?' I gasped.

'Well, madam,' said the policeman, 'after we found him, we put his name through the computer and found that he is wanted in respect of certain non-payments of maintenance to his wife. So I'm afraid we shall have to take him down to the station with us.'

So, after all that, at four o'clock, we still had no taxi for Frankie. We were all getting desperate, so we pleaded with the police and in the end they offered to take Frankie and Betty down to the police station and they could order a taxi from there, which would be easier than having another taxi come out to us because we are a little bit out of the way.

So Frankie and Betty said goodbye, and the last thing I saw of him that night was his face through the back of a police van, with two Alsatians giving him ever such dirty looks!

Even that wasn't the end of it. Later in the morning, just before we left for the airport, he phoned us up to say he'd only just got home! When they'd tried to get a taxi at the police station, no-one would come out at that hour, and Frankie had to wait in the nick with his sister until after seven o'clock.

Bobby and I were still laughing about Frankie's night when our plane landed in Spain. Some years ago we bought a villa there, on the Costa del Sol, and for us it's a great retreat. No phone – it's the last place I'd want one because I actually hate the phone and only use it for business. If I want to talk to someone, I always try to meet them face to face.

When I want a week alone with Bobby and the boys, and no interruptions, the villa is ideal. We have our own pool, and there is a big indoor pool up the road where the boys sometimes go with Penny, and there's plenty of tennis courts as well. Another good thing, from the point of view of privacy, is that most of the villas on our estate are owned by Germans and Swedes, who don't know me, so if I really want to hide and be quiet for a few days, I can.

One day I was queueing up in my shorts and sunglasses at the mobile van which comes round every day with the groceries, and I got talking to the feller who had the villa opposite ours. We had watched it being built, and now it was occupied by this German feller and his friend. He obviously didn't know me, but he'd seen where I lived, so I expect he thought I was renting it.

'Oh, yes,' he was saying, 'that villa is very beautiful. I swim a lot in their pool. It belongs to the Artiste, you know.'

'Great,' I thought to myself, 'it's a good thing we come down here occasionally, so we can find out what's going on.' Aloud I said to him:

'I am the Artiste.'

Well, his face dropped. I almost felt sorry for him. I said: 'Don't worry. You use our pool. I don't mind if you swim in our pool when we're not there.'

Our travels in Spain and around the world have got the boys used to sitting in restaurants and they've become very adventurous in the things they order. You won't find many British kids under the age of ten ordering squid; our Ben was doing it when he was three. At the same age, or thereabouts, our Robert was into veal escalopes, and our Jack, who's still only four, asked if he could try steak tartare. He didn't like it, but at least he gave it a go. While he was still a toddler, our Robert loved garlic – so he wasn't the ideal baby to lean

131

over and kiss just after lunch, because he reeked of the stuff!

****

When I think of warm climates and holidays – and eating habits – I also think, funnily enough, of Ringo. He is one of our oldest friends, from when we were all in Liverpool, and we've been together on a couple of memorable holidays in the South of France.

The first time, he invited Bobby and me to join him, his first wife Maureen and some others(!) on a yacht he'd chartered for the Cannes Film Festival. John Lennon had two films showing at the festival – one was called *Erection* and the other was *Imagine*, and they were kind-of forerunners to all the pop and rock videos which you see today.

I said: 'We'd love to come. But do you mind if we check into a hotel because I get sick just going over to New Brighton on the *Royal Iris,* never mind floating about in the Mediterranean.'

'No,' he said. 'Of course not.'

So we flew down to Nice, went to our hotel in Cannes and then set about looking for Ringo's yacht, the SS *Marala*. We got into a taxi with some overnight things, in case we wanted to stay on board, and went to the new marina. We drove all the way along it without seeing Ringo's boat anywhere. We went to the Port Control office and they suggested trying the old marina at the other end of town. So we drove down there, and by then we were beginning to wonder if we were ever going to find it, or perhaps we were having our legs pulled. We reached the old port and started asking again. At last we found someone who directed us to a very smart boat where a uniformed feller was standing on the quayside.

He saluted us, we gave him our bags, paid the taxi and got on the boat. On the deck there was no-one else in sight. 'Where is Mr Starr?' Bobby asked, thinking the others must all be downstairs.

'He's on the yacht,' the feller said, and pointed out to sea at this great big liner. So we weren't on the proper boat at all. This was the launch!

We drove out to sea, and were ushered on board the sixth largest privately owned yacht in the world. An amazing boat, it had a crew of twenty-two and five launches like the one which brought us, and at night when it was lit up you could see it for miles.

They had three dining rooms on board, but Ringo's party was breaking the chef's heart. Ringo and Maureen were vegetarians and ate very little, even if it was vegetables. George Harrison was there, and he was a very fussy eater, and so were Marc Bolan and his wife Joan. Bobby and I were the only

132

gannets in the place – and the only meat-eaters. Whenever the chef came to us and we said yes, we'd love it, his eyes used to light up as if he'd won the pools. We made all those hours he spent in the market worthwhile, because every morning he used to go down there and buy beautiful fresh vegetables, fish, meat – and until we turned up he had no-one to cook it for.

All Ringo seemed to want was chips. 'That's *pommes frites* to you,' he told the chef, 'not chips, because those are crisps in your language.'

In fact, the chef and the bar staff were under orders to provide chips (*pommes frites*) with everything. And not just for Ringo; for everybody. So if you were lying on deck and you ordered a drink, it came with a big plate of chips. A lot of weight was put on during that holiday!

We took a trip in the yacht to St Tropez. I bought a lovely denim jacket, very French, with studs on it, and a pair of blue jeans. We spent the day there, and then we sailed back to Cannes. Well, the weather on the return trip was *dreadful!* As we came round the headland, the yacht was going up and down and water was pouring over the deck. In the main saloon, where we were all sitting or lying about, the paintings – original masterpieces – were bouncing against the walls – smack! boing! – while our friends were going gradually green and disappearing until only Bobby and I were left. Bobby was lying flat on a sofa reading a book, so he didn't suffer so much from the pitch and roll, and I was fixing the hem on my new jeans, so I didn't notice anything.

The next day, we compared notes. The others all admitted they'd been sick, then Bobby explained that lying on the sofa had probably saved him.

'But I'm surprised at Cilla,' he said, 'because she usually doesn't last five minutes on a boat.'

Then we looked at the hems I'd been stitching on my jeans. Well, they were up here, down there, like a load of hairpin bends on a mountain. Ah, the powers of concentration. At least they saved me from a nasty night.

We had a lot of laughs on that trip, and we even got a song written. Ringo was writing one for me called *Photograph,* and everyone on board was chipping in with bits for it. I was very pleased. I thought: 'This is lovely. Here we are all working together, and when I get back home I'll have a new song to record.'

It all worked out very well, and I really liked it. When it was time to go, I said to Ringo: 'That song is great. Will you put it down on a demo and send it to me?'

He said: 'No, it's too bloody good for you. I'm having it myself.'

And he did. He recorded *Photograph*, and it was a hit. To be fair, he did send me another one, called *Back Off Boogaloo*. But, there again, he did it himself and he had another hit.

That was a planned holiday with Ringo. Another year, when Robert was about fourteen months, we went to Antibes and stayed at the Eden Roc, which is one of the best hotels on the coast. From the hotel a long driveway leads down to the restaurant and the pool area which is built into the rock (that's where the hotel's name comes from). One day Bobby and I were pushing Robert in his pushchair down this driveway when we heard a rustling in the bushes. We took no notice but then, a few yards further on, there was more rustling – and out jumped Ringo, roaring like a lion and waving his arms.

He had taken a cottage in the hotel grounds, quite by coincidence at the same time as we were staying in the main hotel. So we all clubbed together and had a lot of laughs. On our last night, Ringo said:

'Come over to the cottage and we'll have a nice farewell dinner.'

So Bobby and I went over there, the Dom Perignon came out, and we all ordered our meal. Bobby and I both had Dover Sole and Maureen ordered some sort of fish as well. Ringo ordered double fried egg and chips. He was only in one of the best hotels in the South of France, and he wanted egg and chips.

The food arrived from the main hotel, and the waiters rushed round serving us. Our fish was delicious. But Ringo was horrified when he saw his order. They hadn't given him chips with his double fried eggs, they'd brought *crisps*. He sat there fuming quietly, because he's really a very gentle person, until he could bear it no longer. The waiters had left, and so Bobby suggested he rang up the manager. From where we sat, we could just hear Ringo's end of the conversation, and it had us in fits.

Remember, he was being deadly serious. 'Hello,' he began, 'this is Mr Starr here. Can I speak to the manager?' (*Pause*)

'. . . All right. Can I speak to the deputy manager? (*Pause*)

'. . . Right. Now this is Mr Starr here. In the cottage. I want you to know that you have ruined my friends' last evening here. You've totally ruined it. (*Pause*)

'. . . Well, because I ordered a meal and only half of it has turned up. (*Pause*)

'. . . The *pommes frites*. (*Pause*)

'. . . No, no, no. It's no good sending the *pommes frites* now, because the half that did turn up has gone cold. (*Pause*)

'. . . Double fried eggs!'

We just wished we could have been at the other end of the line as well, and seen the expression of the deputy manager. 'Sacre bleu! Double fried eggs. Ow can you ruin an evening wiz double fried eggs!'

✳✳✳✳

I've enjoyed telling you about some of the things we get up to with our friends, and how we live together as a family. You know how they say that the young hold the key to everything? Well, I still don't feel that old myself, but I'm going to let our Jack have the last word, and that will give you some idea of what to expect from the next generation of Willises.

On a hot day, a short while ago, our Jack had got himself an ice-cream lolly. He was walking across the kitchen with it, when it suddenly fell out of his hands onto the floor. Before he could do anything Hazel, our Briard, came and woofed it up.

You could see she was pleased with herself, and it must have been really refreshing for her on such a hot day. But it infuriated our Jack. He was very upset about it. Then, suddenly, I turned my back for a second and he'd gone missing.

Five minutes later, in he came from the garden with a big smile on his face.

I thought: 'He looks very happy for a child who's just had his ice-cream lolly pinched.' So I asked him where he'd been.

He said: 'I've shown that Hazel.'

'What do you mean?' I asked him.

He said: 'I've got my own back on Hazel. I've just drank her water.'